MW01109942

JUST FOR THE
GIFT OF THE THERAPY DOG

"Deanna Klingel is a caring, honest, and talented author with a gift that transports the reader quickly, credibly, and emotionally into the realm of miracles that therapy dogs provide daily to those in need. Lily and Jessie's innate, non-judgmental understanding and memory of what each patient requires, properly positions them as the heroines of Deanna's writing."

> —**Steve Willet**, founding "godfather" of World Canine Freestyle Organization and 37 years professional experience in the world of dogs.

"Everybody loves a good dog story, and here are a bunch of great ones, about love and kindness on four paws. Don't miss them!"

> —**Robert Siegel**, author of *All Will Be Revealed*, and *All the Money in the World*; professor, University of North Carolina-Wilmington.

"Wonderful Book! I was inspired by how many folks benefit from the sharing of these dogs. Therapy dogs possess unique qualities that enable them to bond with people who are going through some of life's toughest moments. Deanna Klingel understands the therapy dog through sharing her own dogs, Lily and Jessie, in this ministry. Her unique and compassionate skills as handler and author enable all of us to share in this experience."

> —**Dr. Clyde Brooks, DVM**, author of *Tending Critters in the Ridges*.

"In describing the people they visit, writer Deanna Klingel offers us glimpses into the aging process, the workings of memory, the importance of love, dignity, and respect with our elderly, and the special bonds that can exist between dogs and humanity. *Just for the Moment: The Remarkable Gift of the Therapy Dog* is a beautifully written book you will want to read and share."
　　—**Dr. Betsy Burrows**, English Professor, Brevard College

"Just for the Moment: The Remarkable Gift of the Therapy Dog" by Deanna Klingel is a work of true inspiration that will be enjoyed by anyone who has ever loved a dog—or ever believed that healing can be delivered by a higher source. I highly recommend it!"
　　　　　　　　　　　　　　　　—**Steven Manchester**, Author,
Pressed Pennies & *The Unexpected Storm.*

Just for the Moment:
The Remarkable Gift
of the Therapy Dog

Beverly,

Our lives are measured in years

But lived in moments

Enjoy them all!

Deanna K. Klingel

Deanna K. Klingel

— 2010 —

First published by Dog Ear Publishing
4010 W. 86th Street, Ste H
Indianapolis, IN 46268
www.dogearpublishing.net

ISBN: 978-160844-656-8

This book is printed on acid-free paper.

Printed in the United States of America

Portrait Photography by Superior Studios, Inc., Kernersville, NC
Cover Art by Steve Daniels

PRAYER OF SAINT FRANCIS

Lord, make me an instrument of Your peace. Where there is hatred, let me sow love; where there is injury, pardon; where there is doubt, faith; where there is despair, hope; where there is darkness, light; where there is sadness, joy.

O, Divine Master, grant that I may not so much seek to be consoled as to console; to be understood as to understand; to be loved as to love. For it is in giving that we receive; it is in pardoning that we are pardoned; it is in dying that we are born again to eternal life.

Saint Francis of Assissi is the patron saint of animals. He chose a life of simplicity, poverty, charity, and humility, and is our model of love to all of God's creatures. His feast day is October 4 and many churches bless pets and animals on or near this date.

ABOUT THE AUTHORS

*D*eanna K. Klingel lives and writes in the mountain resort of Sapphire Valley, NC. She is a member of North Carolina Writer's Network, Society of Childrens' Book Writers and Illustrators, American Christian Fiction Writers, and Royal Scribblers of Cashiers.

Lily has competed in Rally, Agility, and Tracking and holds titles in Freestyle, and CGC. She is third level of advancement for Therapy Dog International, TDIRVA. She's a library Reading Buddy. She enjoys swimming, fishing, and bird watching. Her favorite time of day is evening with everyone in the same room, cuddled on the sofa watching a movie with her eyes closed. She is nine years old.

Jessie probably competed in Conformation and Obedience in her former life, and currently holds titles in Freestyle, and CGC, and is also a library Reading Buddy. She is second level of advancement for Therapy Dog International, TDIAOV. She loves water and soft things that she can carry and riding in the golf cart. Her favorite time of day is when Dave is at home. She is 14 years old, and was recently diagnosed with leukemia.

All three authors wear bandanas that say, *"Life Is Good,"*© because it is.

Grateful Acknowledgements:

*D*eanna, Lily, and Jessie have many friends to thank:

The wonderful trainers we've worked with, whose knowledge and skills have nurtured these small miracles: Denise Call, Nancy Davis, Jan Fridge, Heidi Coppotelli, Donna Ball, Beverly Blanchard, Jane Finneran, Duff and Jane Lueder.

In memoriam, trainers Tino Coppotelli and Melissa Hensley.

Thanks to the members of Western Carolina Dog Fanciers, whose encouragement and friendship helped us through convalescing and puppyhood simultaneously, and introduced me to the wonderful world of dogs.

Thanks to World Canine Freestyle Organization, who taught us to have fun dancing, and how to share the joy of that special bond.

Thank you to Foothills Golden Retriever Rescue for Jessie and all the wonderful dogs they place in forever homes every year. Some of them become therapy dogs.

In grateful appreciation to all the health care facilities that graciously invite us and trust us to visit and share the gift of the therapy dog with their patients and clients.

To Dr. Mark Thompson and his associates at the Brevard Animal Hospital who manage the health care of my dogs. Thank you so much for your kindness and medical expertise.

To Dave, who agreed to have a dog, loves us all, and always supports our doggone adventures. A big slobbery kiss and thank you.

Thank you to editor Steven Manchester, for his kind words, and publisher Mark Jackson for his enthusiasm for the project.

And last, but certainly not least, the wonderful patients, residents, and clients whose stories are told in our book. You have all enriched our lives.

DEDICATION

CANDY

"He is very imprudent, a dog; he never makes it his business to inquire whether you are in the right or the wrong, never asks whether you are rich or poor, silly or wise, sinner or saint. You are his pal. That is enough for him."

—Jerome K. Jerome

CONFIDENTIALITY, PRIVACY, & INTEGRITY

*C*onfidentiality, privacy and integrity, are terribly important. Our volunteer status requires it, our Therapy Dog licensing depends on it, and my conscience demands it. The confidentiality and privacy of the people in these stories haven't been compromised. All the names are fictional; none of the institutions visited are identified. The people and their situations aren't the focus of these stories. The stories are about the magical moments of connection to life through the therapy dogs. And to that end, I endeavored to tell these stories with integrity.

The intent of the book is to bring greater understanding to the work the therapy dogs do. Perhaps it will inspire facilities who use therapy dogs to use them in creative and new ways and encourage staff to become more interactive. Facilities whose doors haven't yet opened to therapy dogs may take a fresh look at ways therapy dogs can benefit their clients.

—DKK

PREFACE

I haven't figured out how I got so lucky. How did I end up with these two gorgeous animals living in my house? How was I selected to be soul mates and constant companions of these warm and loving creatures? I'm so grateful for all they've taught me. How was I so blessed? About the time my husband and I were deciding that empty nesting was fun, I was diagnosed with Lyme disease. The illness and treatment dragged on for five years.

During this time, I met a golden retriever. Even though touching anything with my hands was painful, I could pet the dog. I could feel her warm, smooth coat without pain. I was able to walk a short distance on a flat surface, and the dog didn't seem to mind that I walked slowly or wobbled to the corner and back. She was happy to be beside me. Because I struggled with words, couldn't keep up with conversations, and slept a lot, I also struggled with feelings of isolation. Candy, the golden retriever, made me laugh with her clownish antics, and she made certain that I was never alone. It was hard to fall into depression when Candy was at the door wiggling, singing, and slobbering, because she was so happy to see me. She was just what I needed.

We stayed with Candy and her family when we went to the Mayo Clinic in Jacksonville, Florida. When we returned home to our quiet log house in the mountains, it seemed even quieter because Candy wasn't there to greet us at the door with her tennis ball, singing, and wagging her tail. The house seemed to echo with loneliness.

That night, I said to my husband, "You know how we never thought we wanted to have a dog? And for all the right reasons...seven children, no time to train a dog, children with allergies, travel...but now, I wonder if those reasons still matter? I mean, the children are gone, and I'm not going anywhere. I might be changing my mind. I wondered if you'd like to change your mind, too?"

"Are you saying you want a dog?"

"Well, maybe. I thought we might study it, pray about it, and consider it. What do you think?"

"Great! I'd like a dog. What kind do you have in mind?"

Beginning the next day, every moment that I was awake, I was on the computer studying the AKC website. I was learning about the breeds we might consider. I learned a lot about many interesting breeds that all have wonderful characteristics. But I kept returning to the golden retriever. They seemed to be calling me.

CALLA'S VALENTINE
LILY OF THE VALLEY

I located a breeder on the AKC website that had *puppies on the ground*. I e-mailed her and we made arrangements to visit. Lily was one of ten beautiful puppies, six weeks old. But, in my Lyme Fog, typical of the disease, I hadn't really grasped "puppy." I was saying "puppy," but when I was greeted at the door by a beautiful, smiling 67 pound golden, it was love at first sight. This was the puppy I wanted; she was the dog I'd been dreaming about. The breeder thought I was kidding, of course.

"Well, if you like this dog, I'll show you which puppy is for you. I have a little female that is exactly like her mother at this age in looks, behavior, and temperament."

I was blown away. Puppy? Oh–a *puppy!* The lovely dog at the door was the puppy's mother, not for sale. A puppy… that's right, puddles on the floor, shoes chewed, painful nips on the ankles. *Oh, my gosh, what have I done?* Puppies are little! I wanted a dog like Candy that I could lean into and hug. I really hadn't gotten my Lyme-fogged brain around "puppy" until now. But it didn't take long for the fear to subside and for love to take over. We went back to Virginia to get her when she was ten weeks old and brought her home to the mountains forever. She was born on Valentine's Day and became ours on Easter weekend. We call her Lily.

Lily did piddle on the floor a couple of times. She did chew up Dave's brand new shoe. And she did make me cry out in pain with her puppy teeth. But she learned very quickly. I look back at those puppy days now and realize that she has been a therapy dog all her life. She began as a puppy to know not to trip or nip. She never pushed through a door, raced on the stairs, dragged, or jumped on me, and never got on the bed. She was always beside me where I could reach her. She watched me and she figured out a lot of things that I didn't know she'd need to know later on. She made my convalescing days a sweet time of bonding and learning.

As I got stronger and more determined to have fun with my dog, we took obedience classes, agility training, (where I fell down a few times), and canine freestyle (dancing) classes. With nice manners she easily passed her Canine Good Citizen test. I think it had more to do with her mother dog's example and early training than her training with me.

I didn't really know yet what therapy dog was all about, but it crept into our lives, and she passed the Therapy Dog International certification test with flying colors. Knowing how much she had done for my own recovery, I wanted to share her with others who might benefit from her gentle presence at their bedside. And so began her ministry as a therapy dog.

LILY

JESSICA LYNCH TOO

*D*ave and I joined Foothills Golden Retriever Rescue (FHGRR). We were so in love with Lily, and we felt so blessed to have her that we decided to help that rescue organization find homes for other great goldens. As members, we got the e-mail that went coast-to-coast to all golden rescuers with the heart-breaking story of a golden show kennel that had been abandoned in a nearby community. Thirty seven show golden retrievers of all ages had been abandoned in their crates. Several were already dead,while some died during the rescue. The survivors were taken by FHGRR. Rescue groups across the nation sent donations of money, medicine, toys, food, and beds. It took thousands of dollars and man hours to rehabilitate the survivors. Foster homes were desperately needed, and we became one of those foster homes.

When I arrived at the Humane Alliance on a hot day in early May, I saw the survivors for the first time. They'd been bathed by shelter volunteers in the county and, though they were clean, they still smelled so bad that it was hard to get close to them. I don't know how those volunteers managed to bathe all of them.

My first reaction was that they were all puppies. No, they weren't. The dogs were shrinking, as their bodies made final attempts at survival. I was given a little dog named Lizzie. She was seven years old and was one of the breed bitches of the kennel. We were to give her a new name, do what we could to make her comfortable, and bury her if all attempts failed. She was 20 pounds of exposed bone. She was consumed by infection, scalded paws, and she seemed to be collapsing in on herself. She was more dead than alive.

We named her Jessica Lynch Too because she was rescued the same time as Pvt. Jessica Lynch, who was in the headlines all that week. They were both rescued from certain death. They were both courageous survivors. We call her Jessie.

I drove home with all the windows opened and one hand over my nose. I lifted the stinking, lifeless dog out of the car and I put her on the driveway. My husband cried. I had tried to prepare him for the sight of her, but no one could be prepared for this. She stunk so bad that Lily wouldn't go near–though she was inquisitive and wanted to check her out. She'd stretch forward to take a sniff and then back away, shaking her head. I took Jessie to my friend's groom shop where she and I worked on Jessie for several hours, late into the night, carefully trimming mats off her infected, torn skin, cleaning and salving her scalded feet–one swollen, infected toe at a time. The little dog never made a sound. She just looked at us or slept. Occasionally, she would raise her head and lick one of our hands. She didn't look much like a dog, but when the mats were gone, she was able to stand up and she could sit. She was so pitiful that it was hard to look at Jessie without crying. We really didn't expect her to live through the summer. We just thought we'd love her for as long as she survived.

Jessie got stronger every day. She was clumsy but determined, and could soon stumble up the one step into and out of the house with Lily. The two of them adopted a strange pattern that puzzled us. Their relationship seemed very odd. We watched this for a few weeks before we realized that Jessie was blind and that Lily was her guide dog. With her guide dog, Jessie learned to travel through the house, the garden, and into the woods. If they became separated, Jessie spun in panicked circles, whimpering loudly. Lily made a beeline to her side, circled her, nuzzled her, collected her, and together they were traveling again, in and out of the house. We watched this in awed amazement. It seems Lily knew weeks before we did that Jessie couldn't see. She was a therapy dog, even then. In fact, she was Jessie's service dog.

Jessie's eyes were treated by a canine ophthalmologist–yes, there really is such a thing– and the expense was covered by the generous donations of dog lovers across the nation. Her vision improved, though it will never be 20-20, or whatever the dog equivalent of that might be. She sees as if she were looking through a sieve. You'd never know.

As Jessie got stronger and healthier her sweet and perfect disposition, her innate character, began to shine golden, and we could see the kind of dog that she had been in her former life. Prospective adopters came to meet her, fell in love with her, but felt she was too old, too weak, or too damaged for their needs. It was becoming clearer to me that my husband was not going to part with her anyway, so we adopted her and became her forever family for however long she needed us.

It was apparent, as I began her training, that she'd been trained for conformation. She was obedient, too. But beyond that, it didn't seem she'd had much attention or fun in her life. She ate it up. With all of her limitations, she was undaunted, behaving more like a puppy than an adult dog. She wanted to do everything. She bounded clumsily through agility tunnels, chased tennis balls, and splashed through puddles. She didn't have much endurance and her hips were badly damaged, but we let her do whatever she wanted, asking nothing of her. She learned to dance freestyle and, though her movements were limited, she loved to dance with Lily and me. She's the happiest, most optimistic dog I've ever met. She passed her CGC, Canine Good Citizen. I suspected that she'd already done that in her previous kennel life, but we were starting over. She then passed the TDI, the test for Therapy Dog International. She embarked on her ministry of shedding golden joy to others, who, like herself, courageously live with their disabilities, infirmities, and eventually–old age.

JESSIE

THE THERAPY DOG

*W*henever I'm out with my dogs, I'm asked questions about what they do, how they were trained to do it, and how they became therapy dogs. Frequently, someone will say that they'd like to get a dog and "make it into" a therapy dog. Other times, people will tell me that they have a great dog at home, sweet, gentle, that would "make" a great therapy dog.

Getting a dog to "make into" a therapy dog is a bit like adopting a little girl because you want to have a ballerina in the family, or adopting a boy so you can develop him as a basketball player. You can provide the training, motivation, equipment, opportunities, and encouragement, but then you have to wait and see. You might end up with a race car driver or a chemist. Or maybe, just maybe, you'll get a ballerina or hoop star. That will happen only if the innate behavior, the temperament, the desire, is there. All the training in the world will not change DNA. But, training of any kind is never wasted. Do it; but don't be disappointed if, in the end, the training is used in another way. Training is never a waste of time or money. For your dog, all training will mean he'll be a better pet, no matter what else happens. For you, the training means you can help him be an awesome pet– no matter what else happens.

Training a therapy dog isn't that much different than training any other pet. They all need basic obedience and good manners. Train, train, and train some more. Beyond that, it's all about the dog.

A therapy dog must be a confident dog. Don't mistake or confuse self confidence with alpha behavior or bully behavior. A good trainer can help you sort that out. A therapy dog can't be tentative about entering a new or strange situation. But, that doesn't mean that he boldly charges in and takes over.

A good therapy dog needs to be rock solid-I mean unflappable. If a metal med cart suddenly bangs into a wall behind your dog, will he bolt or will he casually take an interested look and continue on his way? How does he react to strangers who have unusual appearances or odd behaviors? What does he do when he's surrounded by sudden or loud noises? How does he enter a chaotic situation? Is he mildly interested? Overly excited? Tail wagging? Tail tucked? Hesitant? Ears down? Hackles up? Growling? Does your dog bark at strangers? Does he lunge or jump on people? Does he hate elevators? Is he protective of you? You can train to modify these behaviors, however, under stress, dogs will often default to their innate behaviors, so you need to know what those are. Therapy dog work can be stressful. Biters, barkers, lickers, jumpers, lungers, and bullies need not apply. But every dog that is sweet, cuddly, loveable and a great pet is not necessarily a great therapy dog, either.

This doesn't mean that there is anything wrong with your dog, or that he is inferior in any way. Perhaps he has thunder phobia or doesn't like men in caps. Maybe he doesn't like to be groomed or patted on the head, or doesn't like tile flooring. Perhaps he's claustrophobic and fears tight places. Maybe he doesn't like surprises. So what? He's a wonderful, loyal, great pet for your family at home where you can control his living environment and help him with those stress triggers. You can't, however, control the working environment of a therapy dog and its inherent stress factors. So, whether or not he becomes a therapy dog, enjoy your dog for what he can do and what he does for your family. He is, first of all, your pet.

The other part of the question was how one becomes a therapy dog. After successfully finishing a couple of obedience courses and your dog is under control, obedient, and mannerly, you'll have a good idea of his predisposition. If those characteristics still seem compatible with the expectations of a therapy dog program, you're ready to take a look at the CGC. This is an acronym for Canine Good Citizen. This is an actual AKC title, and one that your dog doesn't need a pedigree to achieve. Any dog that can pass the CGC test may attach the title to his name: Buster, CGC. While the CGC by itself is not necessarily a prerequisite to Therapy Dog certification, the ability to pass it most definitely is.

There are ten requirements to the CGC test. You can find them on the AKC website. If you can pass the test, and you and your dog are both still enjoying the journey, then you might move on to therapy dog certification. There are three national certifying agencies: Therapy Dog International (TDI), Therapy Dogs Incorporated, and Delta Society. (There are also some smaller local organizations.) All three agencies provide testing, registration, support, and insurance. Generally speaking, all of their tests are comprised of CGC requirements, plus their own additional requirements, followed by their own organization's rules to which one must adhere. In addition, therapy dogs must always be clean and well-groomed. The requirements are designed to demonstrate that your dog's behavior will be safe and appropriate in medical facilities, elder care facilities, children's facilities, schools, crisis centers, and anywhere else you go.

Basically, your dog will demonstrate that he is able to walk pleasantly and steadily beside you through a chaotic crowd of surprises. You may encounter skate boarders, bikers, children with ice cream cones, basketballs bouncing, strollers, wheelchairs, walkers, canes, –even Halloween masks. There may be people running into you, strangers in hats or wearing tool belts, people reaching out for you or your dog, garbage can lids banging, chairs falling over, whistles blowing, fire alarms, people yelling or arguing, and food trays on the floor. All the while you and your dog will be walking among them on varying surfaces, looking alert, interested, but non-reactive, and your dog will sit whenever you ask him. Many really wonderful dogs that are great pets can't do this. Let's be honest–there are some humans who might have trouble doing this. And that human side is a big consideration. Your dog isn't going to do this work by himself. You're going to transport him, fill your calendar, use your gas, and spend your time on the other end of the leash visiting strangers. If therapy dog work, that is–visiting the debilitated, elderly, confused, hurting, and sick of all ages–isn't comfortable for either one of you, then don't do it. It has to be enjoyable for both of you, or what's the point? You got your dog to enjoy him. From the human standpoint, this work is a ministry.

Therapy dog is an important program that has tremendous value and benefit for lots of people. It needs to be entered into only after careful consideration. It's important that it be the right fit for your dog and for you. Enlist the help of a qualified trainer.

Lily and Jessie are but two of hundreds of certified therapy dogs of all breeds, mixes, and sizes who use their innate behaviors, kindly dispositions, canine intuition, and a variety of trainings to accomplish small miracles and bless lives every day across the country.

GOING TO WORK

*L*ily and Jessie have had some amazing experiences. And I, on the other end of the leash, have been blessed by those experiences. We've met some wonderful people in our therapy dog work who've made us laugh and cry. They've shared their life experiences and enriched ours. They've loved my dogs. I'm privileged to have shared the dogs with so many people who've benefited from their visits, and now to be able to share some of those experiences with you.

Therapists for humans use the words "relate" and "relationships." Dogs, of course–not speaking English as their first language–don't know what those words mean. But, they certainly know how to do it. And it's so easy for them. They never worry about saying the wrong thing at the wrong time. They never have an awkward moment, or that uncomfortable silence. They approach everyone smiling and wagging, assuming the best, offering their simple gift of acceptance, and receiving it in return. They help fill in the blanks for those who've forgotten. They sharpen and refresh fading memories, salve loneliness, and offer a pleasant distraction from unpleasant circumstances. There is no apology in a dog's world and nothing to forgive. Dogs embrace each moment as it presents itself. Life is so simple for dogs.

Embracing the moment is exactly what they do, and nothing is as important to a dog as this very moment. A happy little twirl with a flash of the tail and the glitter of a fancy collar brightens the day of the loneliest person, even if just for that moment. Does it matter if tomorrow they won't recall that the dogs were there? No, it doesn't matter. It's just for this moment that the dogs are there for them and with them.

Lily visits hospitals, adult day care, rehab centers, Alzheimer's units, assisted living facilities, and long-term care centers. Both dogs have been invited to nursing homes, schools, head-starts, libraries, and camps to comfort, visit, educate, encourage, or entertain. We primarily visit in a four-county area, but have gone beyond that on occasion, even out-of-state.

Jessie used to visit assisted living and nursing centers, too, but now she's semi-retired at age 14. I don't ask her to put up with the chaos of nursing homes, or lots of walking in hospitals. But, Jessie still has a lot to give. She visits at a free dental clinic, lowering blood pressures and relieving the stress of the clients and staff. She listens to children reading at libraries and she visits in private homes, where she brings joy and brightens the last days of hospice patients.

Come to work with us now and we'll share with you some of the moments that have been special, memorable, or healing. These moments aren't scientific or anybody's data. I can't explain them and I don't try. They aren't long or detailed stories that need medical conclusions. They are short stories of human-canine connections that somehow make a difference. These are real people, real dogs, and real moments. I don't offer you conclusions or interpretations, but I'm sure that these little moments will touch your heart strings and provide you with some ah-ha moments.

LOLA

*S*he sat in her wheelchair in the hall, accosting employees, visitors, and other residents. Anyone she could reach out and grab; anyone within hearing, heard her calling. "Hey, I have to get home. Will you take me home? I've got to get out of here. They won't let me go and I have to get home. Please take me home. I have to get home."

Her agitation set the personnel in motion preparing her medication. They wheeled her down the hall and tried to calm her down.

"But I *must* go home!"

"Aw, Lola, don't you love us anymore? C'mon, Lola, let's go somewhere quieter, okay?"

All of this was in process when she spotted my dog approaching down the hall.

"Oh, Molly, you came! Oh, Molly, come see Mama." With tears tumbling down her wrinkled cheeks and her arms outstretched, she embraced my dog. Lily moved herself to the front of the wheelchair and rested her head on Lola's lap.

"Look who's here," she called to the nurse. "It's my Molly, and she's come to see me. Oh, Molly, I've been so worried about you, Darling. They wouldn't let me go home to feed you and let you out, and I've just been frantic with worry about you. Oh, Molly, I've missed you so much. But, you look just fine, Molly."

Lily sat patiently, while Lola ran her fingers up and down the canine spine–as if she were an experienced AKC judge. When her hands came to the leash, she looked up and noticed me for the first time. She was wrestling the leash from my fingers.

"Have you been taking care of my Molly for me?"

"Yes, of course," I answered. Technically, that was true since Molly was Lily.

"Well, thank you for bringing her to me. That was kind of you. What day is this?" I told her it was Tuesday.

"Do you feed Molly on Tuesday?" She was getting more distracted, and Lily's leash was getting shorter.

"How about I hold this for you, while the nurse helps you to your room," I suggested. It took the firm nurse to free the leash from Lola's gnarled, but still determined fingers.

"Oh, Molly, what will we do? They won't let me come home to take care of you." The sedative was taking hold and her slurred words slipped into drug-induced snoring. Lily and I moved on down the hall.

The following week when we came back, Lola had a visitor. We tried to slip past her door unnoticed, but the visitor spotted us and came into the hall.

"Are you the lady who visited Lola last week with the dog?" I nodded. She took my elbow and moved down the hall with us.

"I see why Lola thought this was Molly. Your dog looks a lot like Molly. I wanted to tell you that your visit meant the world to Lola. She's been so upset and worried about not being home to care for Molly. Some days, she's frantic trying to escape to go feed Molly. Thank you so much. Your visit reduced a lot of stress for her."

"You're welcome. Are you caring for Molly, then?"

"Oh dear, no. Molly's been dead, oh, I'd say about seven years now. She was an old dog, and Lola had her for a long time. Molly died just before Lola got...you know...sick."

DOROTHY

*W*hen we walked into the dimly lit room, I could see the blips and bleeps on all of the monitors. I asked if she'd like a visit from the therapy dog and she responded enthusiastically. I looked at all the pieces of equipment that were attached to this tiny, frail person: IV's, catheter, heart monitor, and blood pressure machine inflating and recording. I wondered how we'd get close enough for her to pet the dog. The nurse sat the bed upright and rearranged some equipment, and Dorothy sat up. She seemed eager to reach Jessie. When she began to pet Jessie, her attention, oddly, turned to me.

"Are you married?" she asked.

"Yes."

"You have a husband? Is he still alive?"

"Yes."

"Is he a good man?"

"Absolutely, the best."

"Then you need to take care of him. You take very good care of him, you hear?"

"Okay."

It was serendipitous that she was petting Jessie and talking about my husband. Jessie and Dave share a special bond. In fact, I consider Jessie to be Dave's dog.

"Harold is gone now, you know. He was my husband for 67 years. He's left a hole in my heart. But, Harold had a dog, too, you know. She was a beauty. She was a shiny black cocker spaniel named Lady. She had the curliest ears, oh my. Oh, Harold loved that dog. She slept right between us for about 15 years. Isn't that something? I miss her, too."

She petted and talked softly to Jessie for a while, curling and twisting Jessie's thick spaniel-like ears, and then suddenly her attention came back to me.

"Do you believe in heaven?"

"Oh, yes."

"Well, I do, too. We have to, you know. Because what else would there be to believe in? I take great solace in that, you know. I can just picture Harold in heaven with Lady at his side. I believe they're waiting for me. Isn't that a happy thought?"

She laid her head back on her pillow, closed her eyes and smiled. Jessie and I took that happy thought away with us. When we got close to the door, Dorothy called out after us. "Remember, now, you take care of that good man. Thanks for bringing Lady by to see me today. I've missed her. It's nice to see her again."

PHOEBE

One thing we enjoy at nursing homes is their tradition of celebrating life. Sometimes, it seems there's a party every week.

"Oh goody, the doggy is here for the party!" Phoebe was all aglow in her neon pink sweater. She'd had her hair done in the beauty shop here at the living center. Her nails were shiny and red to match her lipstick, which was slowly leaking out of the lip line. She wore her pearls; I'd never seen her without them. Her purse was over her arm. She carried her walker more than she pushed it and she was raring to go. Miss Phoebe loves a party.

"Come on, doggy dear, we're going to be late." Lily and I did an about face and hustled down the hall with her and all the other ambulatory residents and the wheelchairs—all heading for the party. It looked—and felt—like a fire drill. Phoebe was managing her purse and walker just fine, talking all the while.

"We'll be having punch today," she informed us. "Our kitchen staff here makes real good punch. You be sure to get you some. Can you and doggy stay for Bingo later? You might win something. Clyde, you old booger, you, get moving or get out of the way. Why, you're slower than molasses on a Sunday, I swear to it. I hope we'll have decorations today. I just love decorations, don't you? We had some real pretty ones on Valentine's Day. Were you here for that party? I can't recall if I saw you there. What were you wearing? Oh, I remember now, doggy danced at that party. Oh my, how could I forget that pretty red ruffle around her neck? It had little sparkly hearts on it, didn't it? Yes, I remember now, how she danced around and around. Well, now, here we are. Let's get us a good seat!"

We moved into the dining room where it seemed everyone was scrambling for that elusive good seat either in their wheelchairs or in the dining chairs.

"What is the party for today, Miss Phoebe?" I asked her. She stopped and thought about it a minute.

"Well, I guess I don't know. I reckon they forgot to tell us." She looked up, and seeing the balloons bobbing on the ceiling, she beamed. Her smile said it was going to be a first-rate party.

The social director pushed in a cart, bearing the promised punch bowl and a big cake with lots of candles. Phoebe grabbed my arm and whispered in my ear, "Oh, Law, it's somebody's birthday. Make sure you get you some of that cake, and we'll get us a Milk Bone out of the jar for doggy."

"Whose birthday is it, do you know?" I asked.

"I don't know, but it'll be somebody's, you just wait and see." She's an expert on parties.

The social director played the intro on the baby grand, and all the cracked, slurred, and hoarse voices from hundreds of birthdays joined the verse of "*Happy birthday to you.*" Phoebe, of course, sang the loudest, the most off key, and with the most enthusiasm. Looking like the Boston Pops conductor, she waved her arms in front of Lily encouraging her to sing along. (Alas, she dances, but she doesn't sing.) But, at the last refrain, Phoebe paused, not knowing whose name we'd be singing. The others filled in the blank: "*Happy birthday, Miss Phoebe, happy birthday to you.*" Her mouth dropped open in surprise.

"Well, I'll be!" She was obviously stunned. "Well, now how about that, doggy? Did you bring me a present? Well, doesn't that beat all?" She cackled and shook her head. They sang it again and Lily danced, while Phoebe clapped and conducted. She made sure Lily got a Milk Bone from the jar and "a good time was had by all." Miss Phoebe was 96.

IRIS, IRENE, AND HETTY

*T*hey put on their pearls, gather their purses and shuffle down the hall to their daily rendezvous point. There are three chairs waiting at the end of the hall by an emergency exit, next to a little table holding their CD player. The CD's and cassettes are in their purses.

"Come on now, the girls are going for a Hootenanny," they announce to all the residents along their route. They always invited everyone, but no one ever came. Lily and I know they are on the way. The girls all wear wrist watches, a bit of an anomaly here, and they won't be late.

"Oh, there she is!" They rejoice at the sight of Lily. "Will you be dancing with us today, Lily? I wish you could sing. We could use another voice." So here we are at the end of the hall again, the three ladies singing along with the Gaithers, the Statler Brothers, the Oak Ridge Boys. Lily dances to great Southern Gospel.

"This stuff is getting boring. We need to get us an Elvis CD."

"Irene, that man is obscene. He's also dead."

"Well, if you think Elvis is obscene, Iris, I don't want to tell you that I'm in love with Tom Jones. He's hot!" Hetty likes to stir things up, I'd noticed that.

I tell them I have an Elvis CD of beautiful gospel and I promise to bring it next week. Lily dances and takes her bows. They laugh and applaud. It's just another hootenanny at the end of the hall.

These little hootenannies, as "the girls" called them, went on for a long time. They used to joke that they were really the Andrews Sisters or the McGuire Sisters, hiding out from their tiresome, adoring fans. But, over the course of months and years, things changed, and as their numbers (three) dwindled, and the song lyrics couldn't be remembered, even their wrist watches failed to get them to their social appointment.

It's quiet at the end of the hall now. It's been a few years since Lily has danced to the Statlers, though we still visit at Hetty's bedside. But, whenever I hear Elvis belt out that gospel, I fondly remember "the girls," and Lily and I dance in their memory.

THE PARTY LINE

*L*ily got a lot of her early training by going to week-day Mass with me. Our little mountain parish is small. Everyone knows everyone, especially in the winter. Lily learned to greet friends nicely; learned that even though she knew them, she needed to wait to greet them until she was instructed to do so. She learned to stay quietly by my side, and she learned her Stay, waiting for me to go to communion and come back to her. She sat in the aisle. As a little puppy, she'd get bored, yawn, and roll over on her back with four paws in the air, amusing the pious. But, she matured quickly. She doesn't go on Sundays, just on weekdays. We leave Mass and go directly to the nursing home where we take communion to a few residents. Mass certainly puts her in the right frame of mind and behavior for the visit, and I always felt she carried an extra bit of grace away with her. And so begins this tale:

"Hey, lady-with-the-dog, what's your name again? Dinah? And I know, this is Lily." Lily's tail sweeps into full motion at the sound of her name. *Let the petting begin*, she thinks.

"My great-niece is Penny. Do you know her? She says she knows you because she sees you and Lily at church. I said she was mistaken. Who would take a dog to church? Do you know Penny?"

"I do know Penny. Small world, isn't it?"

"Now, why would Penny see your dog at church?'"

I explained the background just as I've told it to you, and I told her how much Lily enjoys going to Mass with me and seeing Penny.

"Well, that's a new one on me," she exclaimed. "Penny's Cat'lic, you know. I'm an Independent Baptist and we don't do that sort of thing." I carefully explained the details again. And following that, Penny's Great Aunt Della was off and running down the hall with the story.

"Maudie Lane, come here. I'm going to tell you such a story, why, you just won't believe this. You know that dog that visits us? Lily is her name. She goes to church in the Catholic Church. Well, that's not something we'd do, but that dog goes to church every single day. Can you believe that? She got trained there."

Maudie retold this story to the nurses' aide. "Yes, that's right. She goes to church every single day at the Catholic Cathedral. Why, she was even born there. Yes, as just a little puppy they say, isn't that something? I guess she must live there."

The nurse's aide discussed it with Maudie and her roommate, and they decided that the lady and the dog must live in Charlotte since that's where the Cathedral is. The nurses' aide has some Catholic friends, so she knew this for a fact.

"I wonder why they just don't visit in Charlotte instead of coming up the mountain?" Maudie told them more of the story, as Della had told it to her.

"Well, perhaps it has something to do with Lily's training, then? The lady said that the dog got trained there, so they probably live here, but go to Charlotte to get trained. Yes, that would make sense, wouldn't it? Maybe the nursing homes in Charlotte don't take Catholics? That might be it."

The roommate told Floyd that Lily had some kind of a grace that she got in Charlotte at the Cathedral where she goes to church every day. Floyd said he used to be married to a Catholic and they do all kinds of strange stuff that normal people would never do, so it didn't surprise him at all that they took their dogs to church. So, he confirmed the story with Della.

Their story took on a life of its own and ended up sounding something like this: The puppy Lily was born in the Catholic Church, goes to Mass every day, and goes to the Cathedral in Charlotte for her training where they give her grace to bring back here to the mountains on Thursdays, because that's apparently something Catholics need to do.

They've all decided that even though Lily and the dog lady are Catholic, they are still nice people, so they won't hold that against them. But they suggested finding someplace else to get trained, since the Cathedral is so far a drive. They said they doubted Baptists did that sort of thing, but we might want to check, since they're just up the road.

They reassured me that they all enjoyed our visits, and even though we're Catholic, they hope we'll always visit them whenever we're here from Charlotte.

Does anyone else remember that game we used to play called Telephone, or Party Line? They still play it at this nursing home.

This is a funny story, but at the same time I find it sweet that they're so interested. It doesn't matter that their story got skewed a bit. They don't have a lot to talk about and they obviously found this matter interesting. They cared that we drove so far to "get trained" and they cared that we came to visit them. They cared enough to offer their noble suggestion to check out the Baptists for dog training.

These folks don't have a lot of resources. They've lost the power to control their own lives. They've no money or things left in their control. But they still care. Caring is a wonderful resource and a gift that can never be taken away. They've taught me that when we've nothing else, when we've no resources left, we can still care about others. And they all care a great deal about Lily.

MARTIN

I paused by the door and watched the jittery man fidgeting with his blanket and table, then the phone and then the water pitcher. I guessed he was a new resident still nervously trying to make this strange environment his home.

"Good morning, would you like a therapy dog visit this morning?"

"A what? Oh, my goodness, well look at that. Come on in. Well, you're a beauty!" Of course, he was talking to Lily. He asked me the usual questions, how old, he or she, name, but his eyes never left the dog. He petted, stroked, talked to her, and was so glad she'd come to his room. He'd just come in this morning to prepare for surgery tomorrow; he loved dogs and had recently lost his. All of this was crammed into the first five minutes of our visit. I recognized the nervous chatter we often hear on this floor from patients preparing for surgery. Then, his phone rang.

"Hi, Sweetie. Hey, you'll never guess who's here in my room. Nope. Nope. You'll never guess. It's a dog! It's a therapy dog, come to visit me. Yup. A golden retriever. Right. Beautiful. Just gorgeous. Remember that one we saw in church the other day? This one looks a lot like it, just prettier. Yeah, even prettier. Hmmhmm. About the same size, maybe a little bigger. Nice dog. Oh, I'm doing okay. A little scared. Don't worry. I'll be fine."

They finished their family business, while he caressed Lily. He was sneaking little goldfish crackers to her under his table. She rolled her eyes skeptically at me, hoping I couldn't see the action. He hung up the phone and told me that it was his daughter.

"I couldn't help overhearing. You saw a dog like this at church the other day?"

"Yes, darndest thing. Lovely dog. Sat there so nice. Looked a lot like Lily, here. Me and my daughter, we got a big kick out of seeing a dog at church."

"Where was that? The church, I mean."

"Oh, just a little church in a nearby town. Nice little church. We were just visiting over there."

"St. Jude's?"

"I believe that was the name."

"This was the dog you saw there. She goes to morning Mass there each week."

"Well, what d'you know. I loved watching her. She's even better up close! Hey, girl, that makes us old friends, doesn't it?"

We visited a while longer. He told Lily about his fears for tomorrow's surgery and joked with her, asking the holy dog to pray for him, petting and hugging her the entire time. I could almost see his blood pressure dropping.

"I'm pretty scared, Lily, girl. You wouldn't be scared, would you? Nah, you're a brave girl. What a good, brave dog you are. Pray for me, will you, goldie?" Lily shook hands with him and nudged the back of his hand with her nose. I told him she was blessing him. He smiled. I wondered if she remembered seeing him at church. Probably–she never forgets a face.

"Come back and see me in a few days, Lily. I'll be better then, okay, girl?" By the time we left, his nervous speech had considerably slowed down and I could see that he was quite relaxed. He felt like he had a friend here. It's nice when you have a friend in a scary place like a hospital.

I turned at the door to say a final goodbye. He had already laid his head back on the pillow, hands folded, eyes closed, and he was smiling. He looked relaxed.

MADELEINE

There is a small aviary just inside the door of the rehabilitation center. The colorful little finches flit behind the glass among the artificial branches for the amusement of the residents who sit in the front room to visit and watch the nest building activity.

Madeleine is usually sitting there on the sofa reading her Bible. She greets Lily enthusiastically, with the soft accent of Augusta, Georgia. She is a lovely lady, who still "puts on her face" each morning, meticulously and elegantly. She uses a rather complicated style of cane, which she says is stylish, and she gets around well. In her life before rehab, she used to hunt in South Georgia with her husband, their Irish setters, and spaniels. Hunting can be very romantic, according to Madeleine.

Even though Madeleine has the high pitched, fun-loving voice that Lily normally responds to, Lily ignores her and goes straight to the aviary, where she sits in front of the glass and watches the birds. Her ears are pricked in alert and she stares into the glass, mesmerized. She sits there, even though Madeleine is making kissy noises and Jack is calling her name. I'm signing us in and there she sits with her leash on the floor. About the time I finish signing in—she seems to know just how long that takes—she taps the window lightly with her paw.

"Hey, birds, just so you know, I'm here. I'm a bird dog."

Lily's family tree displays many champion field retrievers. The only field work Lily has done is tracking, which she loves. But, remember what I said about DNA? Goldens were bred to retrieve birds. Nothing will change that in Lily.

Madeleine appreciates Lily for who she is. She sits with Lily's head in her lap and tells her hunting stories from long ago when she was young and the countryside around Augusta was open and unspoiled. Apparently, she and her husband owned a lot of it.

Madeleine enjoys giving Lily drinks of water out of paper cups from their water cooler. She laughs and acts surprised when water slops over her velour jogging suit. Then, she tells us who she thinks we should "make a point to visit today;" who would like to see Lily. Madeleine knows who is depressed or not feeling "up to snuff". She must make her rounds in the morning before we arrive. I think she knows everyone here.

One time, while she had Lily's attention, I told her, using my Lily voice, the closest encounter Lily had with birds in the wild was nearly disastrous when she followed mallards into the middle of a big lake. Someone in a pontoon boat, who had a golden on board and probably understood the situation, intercepted her and guided her back across the lake to me. Madeleine laughed hard and thought that was the best story. She told me that the mallards must have had a nest on shore because that was how they protected the nest.

"They've been known to drown dogs by exhaustion," she said. She knew a lot about field and water fowl, and a lot about the dogs bred to hunt, point, flush, and retrieve them. She enjoyed sharing her knowledge of bird dogs with everyone in the room. She taught all of us. Madeleine herself had been a champion huntswoman, and reliving those adventures with us was a special sort of therapy for her. There was joy in her telling.

Madeleine always says to Lily, "Now, you come see me again, you beautiful bird dog."

Lily refreshes a lot of memories for Madeleine that had probably lain dormant since her hunting partner died and she was moved into this facility, where there aren't many who appreciate such hunting and waterfowl stories and her knowledge of dogs. We hear a lot of stories about her favorite dogs, while visiting Madeleine. Lily provides a unique therapy for Madeleine. She listens, grins appreciatively at her, and returns to the finches. *Tap, tap*: "Hey, birds, just so you know, the bird dog will be back." Lily's dog parents would be proud.

MEMORIES

No wonder there are so many songs, poems, and stories about memories. *Sweet, sweet, the memories you gave to me…*Just the thread of a happy memory is something to hang on to when everything else seems to be unraveling. Lily gave that thread to Madeleine, and to many others. We've visited many folks who can't remember whether they've had breakfast, but they can remember a dog from their life before this one.

I notice that remembering names seems to be the first difficulty we have with memory loss. Even those of us who are still healthy–once we pass that golden age divide–start stammering and puzzling.

"Honey, you know that guy we used to see at the post office from Memphis who drove that Mustang convertible and had the dog named Barkley? Used to work for AT&T? Remember him? What is his name?"

The accommodating thing about memories for the very old is that no one else is around to remember for them, so they can sort of remold, reshape, retell, and remember all over again, any way they want to remember it. My 86 year-old dad has rewritten World War II history many times. What does it matter? The important thing is that it's a memory to fill the void. It makes me think that Rene Descartes' philosophy "I think, therefore I am," isn't quite complete. I think there's more. "I have a remembrance, therefore, I was." I'm always very surprised how many people with failed memories can come up with the name of a dog from a distant past.

DAN

*D*an was one of the first visitors that Lily had as our new puppy. He lived on the street behind us. We'd never met before, but he was out for a walk down our dead-end road. He saw me sitting on the stoop playing with my little puppy and he walked on down the driveway to meet us. He was a dog lover who'd always had dogs, and currently had two from the shelter. We hit it off. I met his wife, who became a lifelong friend. Dave and I spent a lot of time with them, including a few days at Sea Island at their old family cottage. Of course, the dogs were all there, too, rollicking in the sand and water.

It wasn't long after one of those trips that his wife noticed some changes in Dan. A short life time later, Dan became one of the residents where Lily and I regularly visit. At first, he greeted me with a smile and always with laughter for Lily, as he hugged her and rubbed her. He looked at me playfully, and I thought then that he knew me, he'd just forgotten who I was.

He still always laughs out loud when he sees Lily and she always greets his laughter merrily, the tail wagging the body. She, after all, hasn't forgotten him. Gradually, those looks of recognition became clouded glances of confusion. As his illness progressed, he began that long decline into a silent and veiled world. It was during this phase of no speech that something quite extraordinary happened.

He laughed out loud, as he always did upon seeing Lily. In the midst of his laughter, he shouted out, "Lily Bear!" It's what he'd always called her. Everyone who heard this was stunned. The nurse stared and whispered, "I can't believe that." Although I don't believe he's uttered a word since, even in his advanced stage, he laughs out loud when he sees her and he still pets her. At that moment, he is here with Lily Bear. Maybe she's drawing out a silent memory of one of his own beloved dogs? Who knows what happens at that moment? But, he always laughs out loud when he sees her. Isn't laughter good medicine? Otherwise, his hands lay quietly in his lap, his chin rests on his chest and he is silent.

DAN

He's strapped to equipment,
built for his predicament.
He sits in the hall,
where visitors come to call.
The dog knows his face,
even in this place.
He was both neighbor and friend,
down the road at the bend.
The dog nudges his knee,
his memory's set free.
"Ol' Lily Bear!" he exclaims.
"But, he can't speak," the nurse explains.
It's the old nickname from long ago,
when to his house the dog would go.
His voice is asleep,
the memories buried deep.
The dog curls her tail
near his metal hand rail.
His cold hand warms upon her head,
now they come to put him to bed.
He looks at me blankly,
then strokes her head flatly.
Their existence lay bared,
in that one moment shared.

DONALD

*D*onald sat scrunched up on the sofa, looking like someone should shout, "Timb-e-rrr" at any moment. He came to attention when he saw Lily approaching and quickly sat himself upright.

"Hey, Donald, how're you today? Lily's come by to visit you. It must be Tuesday, right?"

"Well, hi there. Did you know I had a dog once?" I nodded. I did know.

"Yep, a real good dog. He looked just like yours, except he was black. Your dog a girl dog or a boy dog?"

"Girl."

"Yep, mine was a boy, too. What'd you say his name was, Billy?"

"Lily."

"Lily? Sounds like a girl name, don't it? How old is your dog? My dog Ol' Petey was like 12 or 20 or something about that. You live around here?"

"Yes, I do."

"I used to live in North Carolina one time long time ago before I came here. You ever been there? Yep, Ol' Petey, he looked just like your dog. He was just about this tall, like just to the top of my socks here. Can't remember what kind he was, though. What kind's yours?"

"Golden retriever."

"Yeah, I think Ol' Petey was that, too... maybe a Heinz 57. You know what that is? Your dog do any tricks? Ol' Petey knew some tricks. Did I ever tell you about the time Ol'Petey opened the barn door and let granddad's bull free in the yard? Ol' Petey, he just about lost his happy home that day, I can tell you. Whoo-ee, Granddad, he was fit to be tied.

"What'd ya' feed your dog? Ol' Petey used to love to eat green apples in the summertime, and I tell you that dog shat more'n the bull did. Your dog ever do that? Eat green apples? Yeah, Ol' Petey, he was somethin' else."

He slapped his leg, laughed, and enjoyed his own stories until he had to dry his eyes. As he talked, he savored the memories he was pulling out. Petey fell out of the hay mow. Petey almost got run over by the hay wagon. Petey jumped off the cliff to swim with the boys. Petey messed with a skunk. We enjoyed the sound of his merry laugh, while Lily rippled under his massage.

"What'd you say his name was again? Oh, I remember now, Billy. Yep, Ol' Petey, he looked just like Billy here. Except he was brown."

A few weeks later, on another visit, I met Donald's son. He told me that somewhere at home in an old photo album they had a dog-eared picture of his dad and Ol' Petey. He said Ol'Petey looked like a cross between a beagle and a Jack Russell terrier, and his dad looked to be about three years old. The faded picture was about 85 years old...about the same as the faded memory.

HAWKEN

*I*n the many years that we've been doing therapy dog work, there have only been a handful of people who didn't want to be "up close and personal" with the dogs. I always ask them before I tell the dog to visit. If they decline, we just move on. It's nothing personal. Perhaps they aren't feeling well today? Maybe they're allergic, or maybe they just don't like dogs? It's okay. But over the years, most have been delighted and very few have declined. But Hawken, well, he's a different story.

Thump, swish, thump, swish, thump, swish. The tennis balls on the legs of the walker soften the sound, as he thumps down the hall. He'd just heard the dog was coming and he was on a mission.

"Where you going, Hawken?" the nurse asked him. But, she already knew.

"Gotta get to the coop. Gotta get it locked down."

"Now, Hawken, we've talked about this before. That dog isn't after your chickens."

"That blamed dog comin' round here again gonna' get into my coop. You keep that dadgumeggsuckin dog out'a my coop, ya' hear it?"

"I hear it, Hawken, I hear you." The nurses do get exasperated with this. I try to help them out by keeping my eggsucking dog away from Hawken. We steer clear of his room and try to avoid him in the hall.

He has attributed a lot of blame to Lily–everything from "messin' in the bed," "bitin' holes in the bed clothes," chewing the cords "deliberate" to cut off his lights, "purposeful" walking in front of his TV so he can't see it, disconnecting his phone, and of course, stealing eggs from his coop.

Somehow, I don't think Hawken and Lily are ever going to be friends. I just tell her, "You can't win them all, girl. It's his loss. Keep smiling."

But, the bright side is that even though he doesn't interact with Lily, her presence is responsible for some much-needed exercise for Hawken.

JAKE

"Could you come again next month?" the director of assisted living asked me. She had invited us to come and dance for the residents. It had been a success.

"You don't even have to dance, if you don't want to. It's so wonderful for them just to have Lily visit. We'd love it, if you could come every month."

So my calendar sets aside a day a month to visit there. We dance, play games, visit, do tricks, and sometimes learn a new trick, while the residents watch the learning process. Occasionally, one of them dances with Lily. We have a photo of her dancing with a retired Colonel, both kicking in unison like Fred and Ginger. Lily was smiling and showing off, while the Colonel was laughing out loud, remembering his dancing days.

In preparation for her visits, the residents' cooking class bakes dog treats cut out with a bone shaped cookie cutter. They are so pleased to give them to us in a little bag to take home. It must be fun for some of them to be back in the kitchen baking cookies, having a purpose. I'll bet they stir up some sweet memories, while they're at it.

One month, I took both Lily and Jessie because they were going to dance together to *Sisters* by Rosemary Clooney. The residents fell in love with Jessie. There is something about her; maybe her white face, maybe her light, fluffy coat and her stunted body size that makes her look like a chubby little lamb, She just melts hearts.

When she stopped at Jake's chair to get petted, he was quite taken with her. He handled her a lot, smiling at her softness. The director was thrilled with his response to her. Jake has little to say, not much expression since his wife died, and he's generally unresponsive to stimulus. He's very depressed.

"He seems uninterested in life without his wife," the director explained. "Sometimes, he forgets that he can talk and his vacant stare would have you believe he's not really clued in to the moment. His illness is advancing and he sometimes isn't sure of his grandkids' names anymore."

The next month when Lily came for the monthly visit, our "audience" was gathered. Silent Jake sat on the sofa staring at nothing on the wall and waiting for "the show." We danced and Lily showed off a bit, and then we visited each person individually. When Lily stopped at Jake's knee, he astonished everyone by asking in a loud voice, "Where's the little fat one?" He had remembered Jessie for one whole month!

In this place, small victories are huge. I took Jessie the very next week to visit Jake in his room. He smiled at her and petted her. Jessie enjoyed him, too, and her plume never stopped wagging. There wasn't a lot of talking involved. They just enjoyed being together. She wiggled and nuzzled. He petted and giggled. It was the last time we saw Jake. It's nice to think that Jessie brought him some joy in his last days.

A MEASURABLE DIFFERENCE

*T*here are so many different kinds of therapy that the dogs can assist with, beyond just recalling memories. The Eunice Kennedy Shriver National Institute of Child Health and Human Development, part of the National Institutes of Health, is putting together a study of the impact animals can have on children and their healing. The *Journal of the Royal Society of Medicine* lists twelve maladies that their studies have shown to be improved by the company of a therapy pet. Dr. Marty Becker, DVM, has an online essay, *Amazing Power of Pets to Heal*, and he lists "17 ways pets help people to happier, healthier, longer lives."

Lily, Jessie and I aren't nearly this scientific. And we readily accept that not everyone is convinced that a dog in a health facility is a good idea. We always ask before entering a room or approaching anyone. But, we've seen the response the dogs elicit from patients with memory loss; some who don't speak or respond to stimulus; deaf, blind, retarded, those who need physical or occupational therapy with hands and limbs, and those who are lonely or afraid. There seems to be no limit to what the dogs' presence can heal. I don't collect data or try to understand it. I just know it happens.

A dental clinic isn't a common place to find a therapy dog. In our little town, we have a "free" dental clinic staffed by volunteers, as well as retired and semi-retired dentists. Many of the clients haven't been to a dentist for a very long time–or never. Many are physically ill as a result of diseased mouths and infected teeth. Others are just plain scared. It's that old white-coat syndrome.

They come into a quiet, comfortable living room setting and first thing that the technician does is take the blood pressure. Most are high, but some are dangerously so, and the dental procedure may have to wait. So, they hang out with Jessie. In this small reception room, I take Jessie's leash off. I tell her to visit and she goes to the client, who immediately falls in love with her. They talk to her, caress her thick ears, and wallow in her luxurious coat. In about 15 minutes, the nurse takes the B/P again and the change is measurable.

"The doctor is ready for you now. Come on back." Then they wink. "Thanks, Jessie."

Jessie goes there one time a week for about an hour which, for an old gal, is long enough. But the hour she spends there is important for the clients, as well as for Jessie. She's a giver, and she still needs to get out and see people. She still needs a job, a purpose…just like most old, retired people I know.

HANK

"*L*et me see your dog. Hello, you pretty thing. I love dogs. My name's Hank. Have we met before? Let me see you, pretty thing. What's her name? What kind is she? I love dogs. I used to have shelties. We raised them. We raised sheep, too. Ninety acres. One time, we had 27 shelties. They all worked. Do you know shelties? Smart little dogs. This is a nice dog, though. She likes her throat scratched, see this? You should scratch her throat, right here, like this. I love dogs."

Between Lily and me, I call this one-sided conversation Hank's Litany. I call it that because every visit, he recites it exactly this way. By week five, I can almost say it with him and Lily knows exactly the point at which to raise her chin for the throat scratching demo. She listens, ears on alert, and at "throat scratched," she tilts her head upward in complete cooperation and smiles. I am certain she winks at me.

Hank's speech therapist has a name for Hank's Litany. It's called something like "an enhanced verbal response stimulus." He also refers to it as "a communication trigger." I think what it means is simply that Lily pushes his speech power-on button.

Hank's caregivers are surprised when they hear this litany. They say he's mostly quiet, without much to say. They tell me that he can go days without talking. We all enjoy Hank's chatter, however infrequent it may be—even if it's only for that shared moment with Lily, his therapy dog and communication trigger.

SPENCER

*S*pencer is a Vietnam veteran that we've visited regularly for several years. His wheelchair is more like a Strata-Lounger or an Easy Boy on wheels. It's cushiony and reclines. Several years ago when we first met Spencer, he wasn't speaking at all or even making sounds. We'd laugh and joke and put his ball cap on Lily. He seemed to enjoy her visits and he always got very animated when he saw her coming. Lily loved the visits. Spencer thought she was nuzzling and playing with him. What she was really doing was Hoovering his seat cushions and clothing for the cracker and toast crumbs that had accumulated there. She groomed him on every visit and he giggled, as if she were tickling him. Well, perhaps she was.

Jessie also visited Spencer a few times back when she was younger. Spencer was so happy and tried to laugh out loud. He hugged her with very spastic arms and fisted hands, trying to bury his face in her thick, silky coat. She was a little too short for his chair. His physical therapist appreciated how far he stretched to get down to her, and how he stretched and pushed his arms out to reach her. He was normally stiff and uncooperative. But for Jessie, he willingly stretched way down. Jessie became his exercise buddy and visited during his PT sessions. I don't know if he ever caught on that it wasn't a coincidence that she always showed up when he was in PT. His hands, which often don't do what his brain wants them to do, can manage to catch Jessie and finger her lush hair. Though holding utensils is still difficult, he can open his fist to spread his fingers across her back. One day, his therapist helped him to comb and brush Jessie. He giggled and grunted noises and was totally cooperative about bending and reaching and exercising his body. He was so proud that he had done something for her.

One day, when Lily was visiting him, the extraordinary happened. He said Lily's name. Quite loudly, and without hesitation, he said "Lleellee." The nurse standing nearby spun around and stared, mouth opened.

"Was that Spencer? Did he say what I think he said?" I smiled and nodded, while Lily Hoovered and Spencer giggled and drooled. It was the first real word he'd said in a very long time.

Now, through years of therapy, he has found his voice. He makes a lot of excited and jovial utterances, though not always intelligible words. But we have a good time, while Lily Hoovers his seat cushions and wears his ball cap. He loves to say Lleellee and Chessie over and over. That's a special kind of therapy for Spencer, probably not found in medical books.

LOUISE

S he sat in rumpled silence in a straight back chair leaned against the wall in the hall, next to her room door. Her old, black, patent leather purse hung from her callused elbow. In her other arm, she cradled a doll. I'd never seen her without the doll.

"Come here, doggy. Come see me." She looked up at me. She squinted her eyes almost shut, letting a sliver of light slice through her cataracts.

"Do I know you? Don't think I've seen you here before." She was vigorously rubbing Lily's head and neck, as she did every week. Lily knows just where to stand for Louise, so the doll doesn't get in the way. Louise studied me.

"You new around here?"

"Yes." It wasn't really a lie. To Louise, I was new. Every week, I was new again.

"I thought so. I know everybody here and I don't know you. But, I know this dog. I've seen it around here before. It could be a stray. Probably a stray. Do you like dogs? I like dogs. I always take care of stray dogs." She petted, cooed and caressed Lily's ears in exactly the same way every week, suspiciously eyeing me the entire time. Every week, she checked Lily all over for fleas.

"Somebody ought to find some food for this stray dog. I'll bet he's hungry. It's skinny. I just can't abide people not caring for their dogs. Well, thanks for dropping by. I hope you'll come again sometime. Now, if you'll excuse me, I have to get ready for my bridge club. I'm going to have some of those pretty little cheese sandwiches. You know, everybody likes those. I've given out the recipe all over town. Pimento, that's the one. Bye bye, doggy. Come again." She picked up her doll, snagged her purse and shuffled down the hall toward someone else's room. Louise and Lily had both dropped in for a quick visit today. Lily was here for a few minutes, and so was Louise.

INDIANA JONES

I call him Indiana Jones. His room is a page out of *National Geographic Magazine*. A long snake skin stretches across three walls. I told him that I hoped I never met the snake that would fit in that skin and he laughed. A wooden chain, longer than the snake skin, is stretched along the walls next to the skin. It's carved out of one single piece of wood; each link is loose and separate, and stretches around all four walls. Derek had carved it with his pocket knife during a long encampment in a desert—which desert, he's not sure anymore. His words are slurred and dragged out painstakingly long and slow, each word separated into multiple syllables. MS. Multiple Syllables. MS. Multiple Symptoms. MS. Multiple Slowness. MS. Multiple Shutdown. MS. Multiple Sclerosis.

Derek is always happy to see us. He's much younger than most of the residents. He still has lots of black hair, his beard is dark and his skin still fits his face snugly. His arms show a past of strength and athleticism. He loved his work as a geologist/archeologist. He points out the pictures and maps on his wall, along with artifacts, announcements of exciting finds, awards, commendations, and notations from his life before MS—back when he climbed great cliffs and crossed the deserts around the world for oil companies. He wears an interesting bracelet that he says is from South America. He says he "schtoll it." He laughs when he says that, so I doubt he really stole it. He has a floppy old campaign hat hanging by the radiator.

"Is that your Indiana Jones hat?" I teased him one time, as Lily sniffed it with interest.

He flashed me a big, lopsided smile. "Yessssss," he rolled out his answer.

Next to the hat is an autographed picture of Jimmy Carter presenting a younger Derek with his Eagle Scout Award. Most of that wall is covered with an arrowhead collection and Boy Scout patches.

Lily changed sides to go to his stronger hand. *How does she know to do that?* His quiet words slurred, but he talked and talked to Lily. Bent over in his chair, he whispered into her ear. He petted her with his tight fist. He spoke privately to her and her ears pricked forward in appreciation. He had her complete attention. I dropped her leash and sat on the edge of the bed. I became a ghost in the room. I suppose archeologists are okay with ghosts, so I stayed quietly invisible, while Lily took in the conversation meant only for her. *He's telling her chapters of his life*, I thought. Lily seemed to be getting it all; she was alert and interested. Very lightly, she placed a paw on his knee. I watched him struggle to slowly unfurl his tightly clenched fist and he shook hands with her. He gave me a crooked, beautiful smile and explained. I helped him lay his hand, now opened on her head.

"Mee an Li lee…wee make a dealll. I tolldd herrr where the treas sssurrre iss and sheee won't telll." And they shook on it. Deal. He chuckled and winked at her with one side of his face. Lily has kept her part of the deal. She's never told anyone where Derek's treasure is.

Derek always smiles at us, but in his eyes I see a warning: *Beware. Pay Attention. Don't take these moments in life for granted.*

DEREK

Another time Jessie and I visited Derek on a Sunday. It wasn't just any Sunday. It was the Sunday of a Masters Tournament. I came early in order to be home in time to watch it. Derek was lying in his bed petting Jessie, but kept turning his head to see the big clock on his wall behind him. When I jokingly inquired whether he had an appointment, he answered, "Yesss. Mass-ter's 1:30." Oh! I never guessed that Indiana Jones was also a golf fan.

We had a nice visit that day, although Derek's speech is slow and difficult to understand. I learned that he had gone to the Master's the year Sevi Ballesteros had won. He liked Sevi. I gave him the sad news about Sevi and that he wouldn't be playing this year, or probably ever. Derek was saddened by that news. "Soo ssaaaddd," he said. "I ammsso sorreee." He shared a sorrowful hug with Jessie.

He pointed to the wall and a large black hat hanging next to his Indiana Jones hat. I finally worked out that Greg Norman had given him the hat. I thought he said there was chalk on it, so I thought it must be autographed. But no, it wasn't chalk, it was a shark; a small enameled pin on the side next to the wall. "His Shark." He pointed out Greg Norman's autograph on the wall. I'd never noticed it before. "From the shshsharkkk." He smiled.

I turned the TV on for him and pulled the blind, so he'd be ready for the broadcast. I wondered who would have done that for him, if we hadn't come. Derek can't use the remote or the nurse call button. I wished we could stay and watch it with him. We oohed and aahed over the azaleas in Augusta, along with the rest of the outside world.

I told him that Jessie loved to ride on the golf cart. He laughed. "Me, too," he said. Sometimes, Jessie takes a nap on it in the garage. That made him laugh again. "Me, too!" he chuckled. "I did that, too, before."

He petted Jessie's head next to his pillow and kissed her goodbye.

"Goodbye to my golf cart buddy," he said slowly. Once again, a dog connected and brought back memories of happier days and better times. He was smiling. "Yeah. I took a nap on a golf cart–just like Jessie. We must be soul mates."

"See you next week, Derek. Enjoy the Masters."

HAROLD

"Well, look at that pretty dog. Ain't you something else?"

"Would you like a visit?"

"Busy? No, I ain't busy, come on in and set a spell. He's a pretty ol' thing, what's his name?"

"Lily."

"Willy! That's a good name for a dog. C'mere, Willy. What kind of dog is he?"

"She's a golden."

"An old'n? He don't look that old. How old?"

"Six."

"Sex? Which sex?"

"Girl."

"Well, that don't matter none, unless you're a dog. How old is he?"

"Six years."

"Well, 16 is pretty old. Willy don't look that old. But he's sure pretty."

This entire time Lily is being treated to a full body massage. I had dropped the leash when he first called her to his bedside. He'd been massaging her the entire time and she loved every minute of it. She looked over her shoulder and gave me a big, silly grin. I'm sure she was thinking, *You can call me Willy, you can call me Billy, you can call me Silly. Just keep on rubbing, Harold. A little more on the left shoulder…aahh.*

Therapy goes both ways. Lily loved her massage; Harold's arthritic fingers were being thoroughly exercised and he seemed to have forgotten the pain.

That night at dinner, I wore my IPod ear buds stuck in my ears with a stocking cap over the top and told my husband to talk to me in a regular voice. He is very tolerant of my doggone projects and never acts surprised. I wanted to know how Harold heard things. How much was I going to miss of our conversation and TV? I missed a lot. The only thing that seemed right was rubbing on Lily and Jessie, while I pretended to follow Dave's conversation. I discovered it's easier to pretend than it is to ask to have it repeated. It's also easier if the person talking to me speaks slower, louder, and looks at me when he speaks. And in the midst of the quiet, it helped to pet and chatter at a dog. I hope I can remember all that.

IDENTITY CRISIS

*Y*ou've probably already figured out from some of these stories that many people who see us regularly think my name is Lily, if they've thought about my name at all. I'm either "the dog lady," or I'm "Lily," or they haven't noticed me at all. I don't care. I really don't need a name at all for this job. This job requires a visibly worn ID, but it doesn't require a title, or even a name.

The important thing for you to know about these stories is that whatever I've named the people in our stories, I did it with respect for them and their privacy. If by any chance you should recognize a loved one in my stories, I hope you understand that the story is not belittling, ridiculing, or making fun of your dear one. These stories are all written in celebration of their lives and to show how they reconnected–even if only for a moment–when the dogs touched them in some way. And to tell you that they, in some way, touched us.

I can only begin to tell all eight years of stories about encountering patients with blank stares, no expression, no light in the eyes, who made no response to staff members or to me, but who laughed aloud, or smiled when Lily or Jessie touched their hand or arm. Through a dog, they reconnected for just a moment to a life they used to enjoy. Laughter is healing, and I believe we've brought some healing and joy to them.

Of all the extra-curricular fun I've had with my dogs, therapy dog is by far the most humbling. Running agility, dancing freestyle, rallying around the ring on a trot, following the tracker in her tracking harness, all required 50-50 input from handler and the dog. We were a real team. I'm the one who usually didn't hold up under the judges' scrutiny. My tee shirt reads *My Dogs Are Handler Challenged*. But when there was cause for celebration, the kudos were shared 50-50. Nice.

But therapy dog work is different. I can feel a pride in their training and I can say thanks when they are complimented. But the therapy dogs are dogs on auto pilot. So much of what they do comes from who they are; their innate being. I'm chauffeur, and I answer questions on the end of the leash. But, I don't have a lot to say unless someone speaks directly to me. It's all about the dogs. They know what to do, how to do it and when, and their instincts are better than mine. I'm in awe of them, and both humbled and blessed to be at the end of their leashes listening to the stories, filling a lonely room with my nameless human body, and watching the dogs weave their magic. My own innate temperament is shyness, so quiet observance is what I do best, anyway. There is no *I* in therapy dog; no ego, no titles. I'm often not noticed at all. It's a humble ministry. I watch while my dogs offer succor in comfort, solace, remembrance, friendship, and companionship in ways I could not. The least I can do is record the experience and share it by telling their stories.

The only time that I've needed to take an active part on my end of the leash was when a certain Maine Coon Cat sneaked into the hall at one of the centers to stalk Lily. It lunged and hissed at her, then ran. Now she'd like to take off her bandana and duke it out with that cat. So, for my part, I keep my eyes open for the cat and steer us down another hall to keep the peace. The other thing is that therapy dogs require the handler to be attached. That's a good rule. Who knows where the cat or Hawken could be lurking! That could be another story.

MARNE

I wasn't sure if Marne's battered speech was a result of a stroke, confusion, or if she simply spoke another language. It turned out to be all three. On our first visit, Marne wrapped both arms around Lily's neck and hugged her. She stayed bent over in that uncomfortable-looking position for quite a while, murmuring into her golden ruff. Lily stood still and accepted it, listening. Marne was saying a lot, but I understood none of it. I did hear the word comfort, comforted, or comfortes, several times. When she was finished with the moment, she was weeping. She sat up and continued to chat with Lily. She occasionally looked at me, but with detachment. Her attention was fastened on Lily.

I was holding the old tattered magazine that Marne had been looking at when we'd arrived. I asked her if she enjoyed magazines and she nodded. I asked her what kind and she told me food, flowers, and pictures. The next time we came, she was looking at the same old magazine. She repeated her intimate visit with Lily and seemed so happy to see her. Again, the word that sounded like comfort was muffled into Lily's neck. I was beginning to grasp that comfortes might be more than just a word.

We came the following week and I brought my back issues of *Southern Living*, a magazine famous for its wonderful pictures of food and flowers. She was excited to receive the gift of months-old magazines. When we arrived for our next visit, Marne sat enjoying her *Southern Living*. This time, there was no misunderstanding. Comfortes was the name she applied to my dog.

After that, I saved all my *Southern Living* issues for her and brought them along. I could tell how many times she'd handled and enjoyed them, as they were quite ragged by the time I brought the next month's issue.

Twice during the five years we visited Marne, one of the nurses that we'd gotten to know quite well called and asked if we could come to visit her. Both times Marne was obviously distressed and crying. On the first occasion, her roommate met us at their room door.

"I'm glad y'all could come," she whistled through her missing teeth. "You know that sweet ol' soul ain't never botherin' nobody, but that fambly o' hers jes talk so nasty to her, why it jes break her ol' heart an make me so mad I wanna spit. I wanter put that boy in a gunny bag and pitch him on outter here. I tell that nurse she gots to call our tharpy dog to come, sos she can put Marne to restin'. Marne be askin for Comfortes Dog. Lily got that calmin spirit for Marne, don't she now? You go on in there now." She wheeled away.

Marne grabbed onto Comfortes and cried into her neck. She was in such distress that the nurse stood nearby. I watched quietly, while Lily soothed the patient, and Marne slowly returned to us. "Oh, Comfortes, Comfortes."

Then one day, I had a different kind of phone call.

"Is this Comfortes?" the caller inquired.

Um. How do I answer that… "You've reached the correct number. May I help you?"

He told me his name. "My ma died this morning and she has some stuff that I think is yours. The other old woman in the room says she took 'em from Comfortes.

The nurse thought that might be you. Does Comfortes live there?"

"Yes."

"Well, here's the deal. My ma is a regular clepto and we find all this stuff that ain't hers, see. She's got a stack of books in her locker that she's probably stole from you. She's always done that and I apologize. It's embarrassing. If you'll tell me how, I'll return them."

"Are you referring to a stack of *Southern Living* magazines?"

"Yeah, I guess, something like that."

"The magazines belong to your mother. I gave them to her every month. She didn't steal them. I gave them to her." I'd had no idea Marne had saved them all.

"My sister'll be glad to hear that. She thought some magazine salesman screwed ma over an we'd be out some money. Why'd you give them to her anyway? She don't read. She's crazy as a coot, why'd she need a magazine? How long did you know her anyway?"

I told him I thought it was nearly five years. Crazy wasn't an adjective I'd ever used to describe Marne. I remembered how she and Lily walked in the courtyard garden in the summertime. I'd wheel her slowly down the path, while she'd hold the leash, taking Comfortes for a walk. I remembered her delight at seeing the arc of rainbow in the fountain spray. She was like a little girl with an amazed look. "Lookey you there, Comfortes," she'd say to Lily. Lily stared at the water, appreciatively.

"'Cheez, how could you stand it? Didn't she make you nuts?" her son carried on.

I remembered when I got permission to take her on a "hike" in a wheelchair all the way to the end of the parking lot to show her a colony of pink lady slippers I'd noticed blooming there.

"Just like in your magazine," I told her. Lily sat beside her. Her hand was on Lily's head and they looked at the flowers together. I took her picture with Lily to put on her bulletin board and she held the leash on our walk back. *Crazy?* I never thought that.

"No. She didn't make me nuts. Is there anything else I can do for you?"

"Are you Comfortes?"

"No, but I'll tell Comfortes you called. You may throw the magazines away. And we offer you our condolences on your mother's death. I enjoyed knowing her, and Comfortes and I will miss her."

"Well, that makes about two of you. Comfortes is like a really weird-o- name, isn't it? Ma used to have this big yellow dog. I think he was the only one of us she ever liked. He was the only one that liked her, anyway. She called him Comfortes. Soon as we got ma a room here, we dumped that sucker—"

Click. I hung up the phone.

"Comfortes, come. Thank you, dear Comfortes." I buried my face in Lily's ruff, needing her comfort for that moment.

EDDIE

*W*hen we first met Eddie, he had a lot of stories to tell. There was a large picture of him and his fighter plane hanging on his room wall. It looked like a John Wayne poster. The young, handsome fighter pilot in his leather bomber jacket, posed by the wing of his plane, looked totally invincible. And he most likely thought he was. There was another picture of him with General Douglas MacArthur. I figured he was close to my Dad's age, but younger by maybe ten or 15 years. That generation has some mighty stories to tell. But Eddie needed to get his told quickly.

Every week Eddie was noticeably weaker, sicker. Before long Lily had to move from his chair to his bedside. Within months, his stories were getting confused, with no beginning, or no end. He never recognized me or knew who I was until he saw Lily. Then he knew "his dog" was there.

I'd only met Eddie's wife one time. It was back when he was still in his chair and going to PT. She came to see Eddie one morning, while we were there. She'd been Christmas shopping. She was a very attractive woman, fashionably dressed, with stylish hair and expensive jewelry. I could see what a handsome military couple they must have been. I could imagine them waltzing around a ballroom in the Officers' Club–happy, and in love. He'd been career military and he was probably married in his uniform–I'd guess in the early 50's.

She seemed agitated and without much Christmas spirit. Actually, no, she seemed angry. I told Lily to wave goodbye to Eddie and we'd come again next week. But Eddie didn't want us to leave. He wanted us to meet his wife and he wanted his wife to pet "his" dog. He always referred to Lily as "my dog."

When we returned the following week, he asked if we liked his wife, and if we'd noticed his wife's anger. I didn't answer. I was sure this was none of my business. I sensed he was going to make it my business.

"Let me tell you a story, Lily," he began. Lily laid her chin near the pillow and got ready to listen. I waited for her in a chair in the corner. As he petted her head, Eddie told her the story of a young flying ace, lots of trophies and medals, who was such a big deal–such a big fish in a small pond–that when his fighting days were over and he had to become an ordinary fish in a fast moving stream, he found that he didn't know how to swim.

"You know what I'm saying?" He checked in with Lily, periodically. So to help himself fit in, he started doing things that he wasn't too proud of.

"Not an excuse, just a reason," he said, wagging a finger at her nose.

Those behaviors became habits that were hard to break. After several years of trying to break free from the hell he'd created for himself, he fell into a deep depression. His wife and children were angry at him for wasting so many years of his life–and theirs.

"You understand that?" Lily blinked. In a drunken stupor, he fell down the basement stairs and did some serious damage to his brain and spine.

"That's why I was at the spinal center for so many years. I had a lot of surgeries and a lot of rehab, in lots of places. But, now it's over. I came here to die. I hope you liked my wife. She's a really fine lady. She has a right to her anger…you know what I'm saying?" Lily nudged his chin.

Eddie was only at this facility for about 18 months before he died, so I guess he had that part right. They held a memorial service for him at the rehab facility. The unit clerk asked if we would come. Lily and I went. Afterward, I gave my condolences to his wife, not expecting her to remember me from our one quick meeting, months ago. She told me that she had asked the unit clerk to invite me because Eddie talked about me all the time.

I was surprised to hear that because he'd never really spoken to me. He just talked to Lily—did she like to swim or play ball, if it was snowing outside, would she like a cracker—that kind of thing. I didn't think he'd ever even known my name. He was all about "his" dog.

"You were very special to Eddie. He told me over and over that when Lily looked into his eyes, she could see all the way to his soul. He told me that Lily could see his soul and that she forgave him. I admit I felt jealous. But, I'm glad that someone could forgive him. It meant so much to him to feel forgiven. I just haven't been able to do that. So… thank you, Lily." She offered me her hand.

"Oh—I'm not Lily. This—is Lily. She was his therapy dog."

The woman looked stricken and pale. "The dog? The dog forgave him? Lily—is a dog?" She sat down hard in the straight back chair. "I…didn't…I thought …" Lily automatically laid her head in the widow's lap, where tears dripped onto her golden head.

I'd never seen tears like these that came streaming down like a waterfall, but with no sound at all; no sobbing, no hiccuping, just tears gushing forth from a deep, dark place where I suspect they'd been pooling for a very long time. The woman took Lily's head in her hands and looked into her amber eyes. The dog stared back, unblinking.

"Lily, you were a better friend to Eddie than I was a wife. Can you see into my soul, too, Lily? Can you forgive me, too?"

Lily sat still as a stone, dispensing her silent, non-judgmental therapy. I felt like an intruder, but I knew Lily would stand there for as long as she was needed, helping the widow through this difficult moment. I took a seat in the corner and prayed that the widow might come to know the source of real forgiveness and peace.

TELLING STORIES

One of the best things about visiting old folks is getting to hear their stories. And we need to hurry and hear them while they can still tell them. When I look into clouded and confused eyes, or try intently to understand an unintelligible but deliberate statement, I wonder how many stories are still locked in there that can never be told. They can share so much wisdom, so much experience, some little tidbit or trivia that could make life easier, answer a burning question, or make more sense out of day-to-day living. They've already been there, done that, and got the t- shirt–as the saying goes. How frustrating it must be to those who can still remember, but cannot share the memories. Maybe it's more frustrating than forgetting the memories? It's so important that we listen to their stories.

NAOMI

*L*ily and I last visited Naomi the week she turned 99. Naomi had a different story for us every week and usually the story came about when something Lily or Jessie did would stir an old memory. One time, it was her name, Lily. Naomi told us that she had met Lillian Gish and had her autograph.

"Most folks would call her Lillian, but I called her Lilly." She told us all about her friend, Lilly Gish.

Once when Jessie visited, we heard that Naomi used to work with Jesse Helms at the *News and Observer* in Raleigh. She'd also heard of Jessie Jackson, but "didn't have much use for him," she said.

"Now, Jesse Helms, on the other hand, finally got his politics straightened out. Some folks take longer to learn than others." She'd spent many years in the newspaper business and knew many people.

Another time, she had asked about the heritage of the golden retriever breed. Then she told me about her family's castle in Scotland, where she used to summer as a child. She wanted to know the most famous dog I'd ever met. I didn't think I'd ever met a really famous dog. I knew some freestyle dancing dogs that were sort of famous among other freestylers.

"Well, did you ever hear tell of a dog named Fallah?" I said I knew who Fallah was. Lily leaned toward Naomi, and we heard the story of when Naomi visited FDR and Eleanor in New York, and Fallah slept on the bed with her.

"I'll tell you a little secret about Fallah," she whispered to Lily. "He was afraid of mice."

Whenever Naomi told her stories, she was stroking Lily the entire time. It was sort of a rhythm and it sometimes seemed that she was milking the story from Lily's coat. As long as she stroked her long back, the story continued. When the rhythm stopped, she forgot where she was in the story, or which story she was telling.

On one visit, she said, "Can you guess how many dogs I've had in my life? I believe it must be about 40 something. First, when I was small, I had Tippy. Then I had…" She remembered each name and more or less what kind of dog it was, and how it looked. How much of what she told me was real, I had no idea, but she was a good storyteller.

I loved her story about the time she met some Cherokee Indians up in Kentucky and they had this special dog with a funny name they'd brought from Louisiana. (A Catahoula Leopard Dog, maybe?) Had she really remembered this, or was she just entertaining us? Of course, Indians conjured up the next memory of when she and her sister saw Annie Oakley perform in a Wild West show. She said Annie was lucky she didn't kill anyone, but then Naomi didn't believe in luck. She said her good friend Charles Lindberg didn't believe in luck, either but the newspaper called him Lucky Lindy and it stuck. "You ever hear of him?" she asked.

So the week of her 99th birthday, she saw us coming down the hall.

"Oh, Lily, I'm so glad you came. Come in, I have something I want to show you." We went in. She smoothed out her afghan, so I could sit on the edge of her bed. She sat in her chair, which she called her Bible chair, and Lily sat beside her, very interested in what we were going to do next, while hoping crackers were involved.

"I asked my grandson to bring this from my cedar chest at home. I wanted to show it to you two." There on my lap was a big, ancient scrapbook with shiny paper covers and yellowed pages. Some things had been glued with flour and water paste nearly a century ago, and mildew was now framing the articles where the glue had leaked out the edges. Black and white and sepia photographs were held in place with black paper corners, now brittle and cracking. A corsage wrapped in tissue paper fell out on the bed and the crisp green leaves shattered like heirloom crystal.

"Oh, for goodness sake, I'd forgotten about that thing. Honey, do you know who Sammy Kaye is? That was some New Year dance! We danced until the wee hours. Swing and sway..." Her eyes lifted upward and it looked like her cheeks were blushing at the remembrance. Her body swayed to music only she could hear. Lily watched her intently, ears forward waiting for a dance invitation to "swing and sway with Sammy Kaye."

There was the newspaper item about the Ringling Brothers Circus train going through her home town; she'd told me about that. There was a photograph of the President, Mrs. Roosevelt, and Fallah their dog.

"Looky here, Lily...a famous dog. He could be your boyfriend. See that pretty young gal there with them? That's me. I'm wearing my pretty beige serge suit. It was quite pricey. Mary Astor wore one just like it. You know who Mary Astor is? I met her once and I have her autograph." We spent the afternoon paging through Naomi's life, while Lily dozed near Naomi's swollen purple feet, keeping them warm with her chin.

"Seeing Lily there sleeping reminds me of sleeping on a Pullman car going to Chicago. I met Mr. Pullman once–or twice, I think. I'll tell you about that sometime."

That evening, I worked on my own scrapbooking hobby. Who knew who might see it someday? I felt so privileged to have seen those old newspaper items and heard about Sammy Kaye. I wondered if that isn't the best part of life; all those little insignificant moments, piling up in scrapbooks to equal something huge or astonishing that most of us never accomplish.

We never got to hear the story of sleeping on a Pullman car. She was 99 and 29 days.

HELEN

They told me she was 104 years old and had just moved in this week. She would probably like to see the dog, so could I stop in, third room on the right.

Sarah Plain and Tall was what I thought of when I saw her. Even though she was sitting in a wheel chair, I could see that in years passed she may have been close to six feet tall. She was walking her wheelchair around the room with rapidly moving, agile feet in about size ten polished loafers. Her gray hair, receding in the front, was pulled back tightly and neatly into a long, silver pony tail with a ribbon around it. Her crisp, ironed blouse was tucked into her khakis that had ironed creases down the front. She was as neat as a pin. She wore a watch pinned to the blouse and a pretty bracelet. Her face was soft and smooth. *Did they really say 104?*

"Hello," I said, cheerfully. "Would you like a visit from Lily? She's a therapy dog who would like to meet you." Helen looked up through her little half-lens reading glasses. She spoke with the clear, smooth voice of a much younger woman. It startled me. It was so unlike what I was expecting 104 to sound like. Lily's tail said she was eagerly awaiting the release to go visit.

Helen invited us into to her "parlor" and offered me the "easy" chair. She offered us both peanut butter crackers, which we declined, and a game of checkers which we accepted. She won. She said she was decorating her parlor and could use our opinions. A tall stack of magazines was piled precariously beside the bed, daring Lily's sweeping tail to topple them. Helen deftly reached over and selected one, without even holding the arm of the wheelchair. A tiny pair of scissors appeared in her hand and she began to snip. They looked like manicure scissors, but she informed us that they were scherenchnitte scissors.

"See there?" She pointed to the wall. I could see the decorating had begun. Bright colors cut from the magazines were stuck to the wall in many shapes and resembled lace. Tiny scraps of paper confetti flurried and scattered about the floor when she walked her chair around. She easily pulled a full page Jackson and Perkins rose advertisement from a *Southern Living Magazine*, with the help of a sharp ruler. I guessed she'd been a teacher.

"Look. See this? What do you see? A white rose? Watch carefully, your eyes may deceive you. Watch now." She instructed as she clipped, and I knew for certain that she'd been a teacher–and she still was. I watched her crystal clear, blue eyes behind the little half glasses. Her nimble fingers scissored away at the white rose; tiny pieces of confetti rained to the floor, where Lily playfully sniffed and pawed at them.

"Now, if you will be so kind as to be the custodian of the Scotch Tape, we shall see what we shall see." I handed Lily the Scotch Tape to carry to Helen.

"Do you think it should go here, or would it look better here? From the bed... or from the door... what do you think?" We agreed on the spot and she slapped it on the wall. The large white Jackson and Perkins rose was now a lacy seagull hovering near the window. It had a tiny eye and feathered wing tips, which she'd curled up on the ends with her scissors. The gull's legs and feet followed the gliding body. I could almost hear it. It took my breath away.

Week after week, we watched Helen create. Her walls looked like a crazy quilt of many colors, many shapes. And only when one took the time to look at each individually would they show you what they were. Yes, she had warned me, your eyes may deceive you. Several of the individual cut outs actually fit together like a mosaic, even though they were all cut out separately, one at a time, with no pattern. One such set was about three feet across and two feet top to bottom. It was a school of fish that had hatched out of many magazine ads for Kraft Macaroni and Cheese. I'd never before noticed that macaroni looked like fish scales. Lily lay on her paws and stared at the art work.

One week, Helen announced that it was National Lily Day. Carefully removing a page of day lilies from a *Home and Garden Magazine*, she called Lily to her side.

"Now then, young lady, this is your name day. You must tell me how you came to be called Lily." Speaking on Lily's behalf, in a little doggy first-person voice, I told the story of naming Lily, while Helen snipped away at the colorful lilies. She said her personal favorite flower was the day lily. When she was finished, she slapped her creation on the wall. It was a lacy, colorful head of a golden retriever cut from the yellow and orange day lilies. "That's all for today, class." I could only stare in wonderment.

By the time Helen left there, every square inch of the wall was covered with her beautiful scherenschnitte cut outs. She had learned the name of everyone on her hall and she knew where most of them had lived. She knew the life stories of most of the housekeeping staff; knew the names of everyone's doctors, many of the regular visitors, and how many children and grandchildren they had. She was one of the few who knew that Lily was the name of the dog, and that I had another name. She had also soundly beaten everyone at checkers.

PAMI

A few years ago, Jessie had a patient that she was especially fond of. I can't pronounce the lady's Portuguese name correctly so I shortened it, but Jessie had no problem with it. Jessie is a vocal dog. She sings and makes vocal noises, sometimes even in her sleep. When you talk to her, she talks back. The only other dogs I've known to do this were Candy and a couple of Siberian huskies in our freestyle group. While Lily is the silent one, Jessie is the jabber jaw.

When we arrived in her dimly lit room, Pami was always sitting forward in her chair, hands between her knees, looking down at her hands, or the floor. It was quiet in her room and I don't think she had many visitors. She wasn't sick, so there wasn't a lot of staff in and out, either. She didn't seem to require any services. I don't know why she was there. Maybe they didn't know where else to put her? She sat quietly alone, until Jessie came, that is. Since Pami was always looking down, Jessie would walk right into her circle of vision.

I don't know any Spanish or Portuguese and I don't know if our friend knew any English. If so, she chose not to speak it. Jessie didn't care. She laid her head on her lap and began to sing, whine, chortle, chant, and apparently did it in Pami's language because Pami seemed to understand every word. The two of them chatted back and forth, even interrupting each other, and with all the expression of two girlfriends having an outing at Starbucks. *Chatter, chatter, chatter*, the two of them carried on. They had a week's worth of gossip to get caught up on. They'd laugh, talk, gesture, all in a language unknown to me. They'd have such a good time. Pami seemed so alive, so animated, so happy, so well, so understood in those moments. Sometimes, she'd slap her knee and laugh, as if Jessie had told the funniest joke. Jessie'd smile and wave her plume of a tail, and it sounded like she giggled. You think I'm making this up, don't you? You had to have been there.

I took communion to Pami weekly, while Jessie sat wiggling through our prayers anxious to begin their visit. When we left, Pami dropped her hands between her knees, leaned forward in her chair, dropped her chin to her chest and looked at the floor in silence. As far as I could tell, she sat like that for the week.

Jessie says language barriers don't exist and I believe her. A hand on a shoulder, a soft paw on a knee, a squeeze of the hand, a moist muzzle on the arm–they all say the same thing in every language. "I'm here. I care. You aren't alone." And in that moment, that might be all that's needed.

CHILDREN, COME!

*B*oth of my dogs love children. Most goldens do, and for that matter, so do many dogs. Not all, though. Children are unpredictable, move differently, and have different voice tones–all matters of grave importance to dogs. So never assume that all dogs love children and want the children to pound, pull, ride them or squeeze them around the neck. Thanks to the current trend of Responsible Pet Ownership and other community programs, most children are being educated as to how to approach a dog. For their part, dogs need to learn how to respond to a child's approach. For some dogs, it's a given. They are so head over heels in love with the small fry that they roll over and act goofy, trying to fit into their goofy world, is my guess.

Holiday times are exciting times for my dogs because the grandkids show up and some of them bring their dogs with them. We usually are about 25 people and five or six dogs. And what a rollicking good time we all have. But my dogs don't regularly see children. We live in an area heavily populated by retirees. Children do visit the resort, and we find them on the playground, or in town eating ice cream. The dogs spot them a mile away. They stand still, tails waving wildly in the air, "Hey! Over here, we're over here. Kids, Come!"

Most children ask, "May I pet your dog?" I thank them for asking and the dogs sit. This must be a tough moment for them. They want to play, smell behind the kids' ears, check out their shoe laces and hope to be invited to their game. But, instead, they sit there politely, tails sweeping the ground. When it's a toddler that's visiting, Lily drops to her elbows to accommodate the child.

Both dogs have enjoyed visiting classrooms, camps, head-start programs, and library Reading Dog programs. But they just can't get enough of those kids. Because of our location and the type of facilities we visit, they rarely encounter them in their therapy dog work. When they do, it's a treat for everyone.

One day, the director of the dental clinic called to ask Jessie to come in when a group of three or four Hispanic boys were being brought in. *Children! Oh, joyful day for Jessie.* The experience of the little boys was highlighted in a newspaper column about the clinic and Jessie's picture accompanied it.

We met someone in town later who had seen the picture in the paper and recognized Jessie. Unfortunately, she had the column and picture for the animal shelter mixed up with the clinic story and picture. She was hoping to adopt Jessie from the shelter for her children.

OUR BOYS

*W*e were expecting a crowd to walk in the door of the dental clinic any minute now. When the door opened, ushering in the cold winter air, Jessie looked towards it, tail already in greeting mode. But when she saw the four little boys, the tail went into a spin like a helicopter rotor. She didn't know which child to greet first.

The boys were surprised and one of them wasn't so sure that this was a good day. He was afraid of dogs. They all spoke English as a second language; some better than others, none too well.

"That's okay, Jessie doesn't speak English, either," I told them. The fearful child, with his arms wrapped around himself, headed for the far corner, where he felt safer from the dentist, the place, and the dog. The middle boy dropped to his knees and wrapped his arms around Jessie, immediately forgetting his fear of this place, while wallowing in her welcoming coat. The other two mustered courage to pet her. It didn't take very long for the fearful one in the corner to join the others and tentatively touch her.

They had come in frightened of the dentist office, an unknown and scary place. It was a first for all of them. Their teeth hurt. The pain kept them up at night and caused them to miss school. So they were looking forward to the end of that nightmare, but a trip to the dentist was as fearful as the pain.

They played with Jessie, her tennis ball, and squeaky toy, which she is loathe to share. Momentarily, they forgot their pain and their fear of the place, while they laughed and rolled around on the floor with her. I showed them how to get Jessie to do things with them and they played with her until it was their turn. The time passed quickly and their fear was soon forgotten, as they crawled around pretending to be dogs.

Their dental work was extensive, requiring several more visits. But never again were they afraid to come. They looked forward to seeing Jessie. A call from the office manager assured them that Jessie would be on duty that particular hour when "our boys" were scheduled and that she'd be there to greet them the moment they walked through the clinic door.

Jessie was their special friend who helped them through their scary ordeal.

LITTLE BUDDY

One day while visiting ICU, the nurses wanted us to visit a six year-old boy. We rarely have the treat of visiting a child, as this hospital doesn't have pediatrics. The nurse had cleared it with his mother and they were expecting us.

When we went into the darkened room, the bed was positioned just slightly up. The mother was in the bed, on the side nearest the door, wearing a white tee shirt, covered up, looking like any other adult patient. From the door, we couldn't see the child at all. I gave a cursory look at the IV stand, the table, the chair. I needed to see where Lily should position for the visit, or what might need to be moved. But Lily, who always waited at my side for her instructions, didn't wait.

She went straight to the mother, and carefully put one paw up on the bed, followed by the second paw. Standing on her two back feet, she stretched herself forward to peer over the mother and looked directly down on a hidden and surprised child. She grinned and looked over her shoulder at me, tail brushing everything. "I found him," she seemed to be saying.

How did she know?

I, the dummy on the end of the leash, was totally stunned. In the seven odd years that she'd been visiting, she had never, ever, put her feet on a patient's bed. I'm not sure that she would comply, even if I had asked her. I'd never trained her not to do this. It's just her sense of propriety. She simply never, ever put her feet on a bed. I respect that, and I've never asked her to do it. Other therapy dogs do put their feet on beds and some get into the bed. It's okay, but, just not Lily's way. But, there she was, with her paws on the mother's legs, smiling down on the little boy. She was saying, "Hey there, little buddy, I came to see you!"

How did she know?

The tickled child giggled and sat up.

"The doggie likes me, Mommy!"

Lily's a hugger, not a kisser. But, she pressed her nose softly against the boy's cheek. He giggled again.

"He kissed on me! I like this dog."

How did she know?

The mom said that the 70 pound dog was light as a feather, and that she hardly felt her paws on her legs. She also said it was the first time since they'd been there that she'd heard her little boy laugh.

Yeah, she just knew.

CAREY AND RILEY

O ne afternoon in the fall, I had a phone call from a senior at a local high school. She was calling to ask me to be her mentor for her senior project. Her project was learning how to train a dog to become a therapy dog. *Hmm*, I thought, *this could be interesting…might be fun. And I'd love to pass on what I've learned to someone so young.*

I gave her the whole background, just as you read in the first chapters of this book. I told her that she needed to take her dog to a certified trainer for obedience training. I agreed to show her how to train for specific therapy dog needs. I emphasized that there was no guarantee that the dog would become a therapy dog. We would go through all the training and she could learn all about it for her project. Then, we'd see what the dog decided to become.

Carey had found her puppy in a badly-damaged cardboard box along the highway. Other puppies inside the box were killed upon the impact of heaving the box. The other puppies that had made it out of the box were killed on the road. This little guy was the only survivor. She stopped her car, picked him up and took him home. She concocted the story about needing to keep him for her senior project because she was certain that her parents wouldn't allow her to keep him. Her ploy worked.

Riley turned out to be a very smart puppy and as cute as a teddy bear. His coat, tail, and ears look like a Bernese

Mountain Dog. His coloring, facial marking and physical structure are probably Rottweiler. He learned quickly and his natural behaviors were stunning. He behaved like a mature dog. Over the next few months, we watched him grow, and grow, and grow. He was totally obedient, gentle, loved to be handled, and had nice manners.

I went to see them once a week, showed a training behavior to Carey who practiced it all week and Riley showed it off perfectly one week later. I taught her to teach Riley to back through a maze. Therapy dogs often have to do this. They weave between beds and chairs, over-the-bed tables, around IV stands, monitoring equipment, all kinds of things, to get close enough to be petted. Then they have to get out without disturbing the equipment. So yes, they need to know how to back up. Little dogs, of course, have a real advantage here. Their handlers just pick them up and put them where they want them. Handling my dog or Riley is like parallel parking a Greyhound bus.

We worked on the wait command, so when they arrive at a facility and she opens the car door she won't have the dog jumping out before she gets her things together and gets the leash on. She will also use this when a facility uses a special code to open a door and Riley needs to wait. We worked on his leash manners; therapy dogs are always leashed. We taught him targeting, so she can instruct him where to put his nose or his paw so a patient can see, feel, or touch him. Riley learned some cute tricks to show off, learned to weave in and out of obstacles in tight places following Carey without fear, and was desensitized for noises. He doesn't jump or bark, and doesn't mind how he's petted or touched. He learned to potty-on-command, a must before going into a facility. And he enjoys being groomed, including brushing his teeth. He certainly was showing great promise as a therapy dog.

I showed Carey my little pack of equipment that I always carry with me on a visit, along with my favorite leash. It's called a traffic lead. It has a loop at the end, but it also has a shorter loop near the dog. Not many people use this leash and it's a little hard to find in stores. But, I use it for the extra control, in and out of tight situations, but also for another reason. This leash allows patients to "walk" my dog, as in the story of Comfortes. They can hold the lower loop, even while riding in the wheelchair, and I can hold the end loop and maintain control. I explained to Carey that it's like a drivers ed car. Children sometimes want to "walk the dog," and this lets me agree to that in a safe and controlled manner. I highly recommend this leash for therapy dog work. We got Riley used to this leash and soon he didn't even notice the lower loop in his vision.

Carey accompanied Lily and me to a Healing Arts Festival held at one of the hospitals we visit. She sat with us at the pleasant booth they set up for the therapy dogs, and she took part in answering questions, while observing Lily at work.

Then one day during her spring break, she spent the morning with us and we visited three totally different kinds of facilities– hospital, adult day care, and a rehab center– so she was able to observe a plethora of behaviors and trainings that are helpful to a therapy dog in varied environments.

Carey had turned out to be a dedicated handler, and Riley was well on his way to becoming a good therapy dog. He needs to be older before he can be tested, but he's ready to take his CGC test and show off for Carey's project.

Near the end of our training on the day she was observing, an interesting thing happened with Lily and a man named Bud…

BUD

 ud wasn't new to Lily and me. We'd visited him on many occasions. One time, we walked down a long hallway beside him. He used a walker and though I wasn't always sure what he was talking about, we had a pleasant time together. Another time, Lily visited him in his room. He'd always enjoyed her visits and enjoyed petting her. So, no, we weren't strangers.

But the day Carey was with us, we walked into the lounge and Bud was sitting in the chair with his walker in front of him. He looked at Lily, made an instant connection, and in an unreasonably loud voice, he shouted, "Bogey! Come on, Bogey, I got to get you out of here."

In the blink of an eye, he had grasped Lily's collar and was twisting it, trying to drag her out by the collar. His other hand was clawing the leash from my hand. He was standing without his walker, pushing me with his elbow and trying to drag Lily out with him, shouting her name, "Bogey," over and over.

Bud is a small man, only about my height, and probably doesn't weigh more than 100 pounds. Yet, he was so strong that with both hands I couldn't untangle his hand from the leash, which was getting shorter. He had grasped her collar so firmly that she couldn't move her head and one of her front paws was being held off the ground as he dragged her. I reached under her chin and released her collar. Carey called her, while I continued to extricate the leash and collar from Bud's hand. Bud was moving all over the place, shoving me. He grabbed my arms, pushed and pulled, and it was not easy to get free. I was surprised to see him so strong without his walker. I couldn't push back for fear he would fall. He was so agitated that he came chugging down the hall after us, as I went for the administrator to tell her that Bud was in trouble and might hurt someone.

Carey was shaken. "Why did he grab you? What did he want with you?"

"He didn't want me. He wanted his dog, Bogey, and I was in his way."

If ever there was a situation that could cause a dog to growl, snarl, or physically try to free herself, this was it. A yelling stranger has her head locked and is dragging her away by the collar, he's yelling and fighting with Mom, and now the dog is free and Mom is being pushed...oh, boy. Lily never uttered a sound. She didn't bolt or lunge. She wasn't even visibly shaken. She obviously thought I had it under control, though Carey and I weren't that sure. I snapped her collar and leash back on and we went down the hall, as if nothing had happened, though we had to flee from Bud a few more times before finding the administrator.

Remember what I mentioned in the early chapters about the unflappable therapy dog? This is why it is so important to know the dog and to test for every possibility.

On the way home, Carey seemed very quiet. She asked me if I'd been afraid and was I worried about Lily. She was surprised that Lily hadn't bitten Bud or at least growled. I asked her what was on her mind. Then she told me this story about Riley.

She said just the past weekend when her boyfriend and other friends were visiting at her home they were playing with Riley, showing off his tricks and training, and all her friends were quite impressed. She was pleased with Riley's behavior in the crowd of friends. Riley really likes her boyfriend, she said. They play Frisbee, rough house, run around, and play fetch. Then Carey and the boyfriend started arm wrestling and messing around, yelping and playing, the way flirting teens do. Riley didn't like that. He took a threatening position, looking like a much larger dog, tucked his chin, and growled deeply at the boyfriend. They stopped their play, but she said Riley kept an eye on the boyfriend and managed to park himself close to Carey the rest of the afternoon, unwilling for the boyfriend to invade the ring of safety that Riley had created for her. Carey was imagining Riley meeting Bud in a situation like we'd encountered this morning, and she was feeling uncomfortable.

Okay, there it is. This is Riley's innate self. This is who he is. Now we know. Riley is Carey's protector.

Carey is leaving for college next fall and hopes to have Riley with her in an apartment. Riley is not an aggressive dog and is extremely well-mannered. He is gentle, sweet, loving, friendly, and playful—and protective. At this moment in her life, he is exactly the dog she needs.

There will be lots of time in her life for other dogs who may turn out to be therapy dogs. Riley has chosen a different job. It's all about the moment—and the dog's connection.

HOSPICE

A particularly sensitive place for a therapy dog to work is in hospice where the dog's silent acceptance is so appreciated. This is where many of us humans would fail without the dog to show us how to just *be* there. Forget trying to say and do the right thing and worry about the foot in the mouth. Just to be there is what is important. Both of my dogs have been privileged to spend the last weeks, or days, or hours of life, comforting and loving people in nursing homes, hospitals, and their own homes. Sometimes it was a sad surprise to arrive and find one of our friends no longer there. But a hospice situation is slightly different. It's more of a preparation time for everyone, kind of a readjustment; a beautiful experience, really. It's kind of like Lent.

In a home that has a pet, the therapy dog is built in, and the owner will take great comfort from his own pet. In a home that doesn't have a pet, a visiting therapy dog can make a difference. A visit from the dog is a happy distraction for the patient and the caregivers. The dog is a comfort, and maybe a relief from pain. Does the pain really go away? Does it matter? We don't understand why all medicines work the way they do. We just accept it. What works–works. And therapy dogs work.

EMMA

The room was hot and humid;
The smell was old and sour.
The blinds are drawn against the day;
A game show fills this hour.

"Lily's here, Emma, do you want to see?"
I asked over the applause on TV.
Emma likes her game shows on daytime TV,
But says, "When you come, wake me, please."

So I stepped inside and spoke her name.
Guessed she was really into this game.
Lily whined in an unusual way;
She's normally quiet the entire day.

"Lily," I said, "go visit Mrs. Cook."
Lily lay down with a questioning look.
My body felt flat, my hands started to shake.
Both of us knew we'd arrived too late.

GRANNY

One day at the dental clinic, Jessie was visiting a lady with a swollen and painful jaw. She caressed Jessie and commented that her wonderful disposition made one "feel happy and forget the pain." She wished her great aunt could see Jessie.

"My aunt is 103. Her old dachshund recently died at 16. She wants us to buy her a new dog. Did I mention she is 103?" We both laughed and agreed that was pretty optimistic.

"Maybe we've seen your aunt. Is she at the nursing home?"

"No, she lives at home. My cousin and I take turns staying nights with her, and we have a caregiver stay with her all day. She does pretty well. But she really misses her dog. She talks about him all the time."

After finding out that she lived in the next town, I volunteered to bring Jessie once a week. We made the arrangements and Jessie began her service as a private-duty therapy dog to a woman known as "Granny."

She lived in an old family home on a road named after her family. Each visit, I learned something interesting about this family. Most of the "old heritage" names from the little cluster of towns here in the mountains are names plucked off her family tree. This family has been around these parts for a long time. Her caregivers, both named Betty, have known her all their lives.

Granny gets around well with a walker and they take excellent care of her. She is always groomed, dressed, and seated at the table eating something, often ice cream, or sitting in front of the TV watching cooking shows, eating something, usually popcorn. She's pretty bright and seems to digest food and information well. But she does have an interesting little glitch in her communication process. I call it her Question of the Day.

She can converse, back and forth, quite well. But then she asks the Question of the Day. "Where do you and your dog live?" I tell her. Then we chat; weather, TV show, then the question. "Where do you and your dog live?" I tell her. We visit, she talks to Jessie, tells me about her dog. Then: Where do you and your dog live? I tell her. And so it goes. The Question of the Day is always a real question: "What does your husband do?" "Do you and your dog live alone?" "Where'd you get your dog?" A real question, but she just gets stuck on it.

Her niece shook her head and chuckled. "Have you ever known a 103-year-old before?" she asked me. I thought about it.

"Well, actually, my dog Lily visits a lady at the nursing home who's 101. She turned 100 the same week Lily made her 100th visit and they had their picture taken together for the newspaper."

"Oh, that would be Aunt Doshie. She's kin to Granny." *Really?*

"One time, at another nursing home, when we were asked to dance with a dulcimer group, we met a man who was 104."

"That would be Uncle Harry. He's kin to Granny, too." *Really.*

On another visit, I admired a painting and heard about an aunt who'd painted it. She lived to be 106. *Really!* We're talking about a super study in genetics here. I'm wondering if her old friend Jessie, now 14, might be kin to Granny, as well. *Really!*

I've learned a lot about life and living from all the "old timers" we've visited. But from Granny's family, I learned the meaning of the commonly used phrases "respect for life" and "living and dying with dignity." I learned that those are more than clichés. Granny's home is clean, her bed is changed, her clothes are fresh every day, and she is surrounded by people who care. They keep a visitors' registry on the table and it looks to me that not a day goes by when someone doesn't come by for a visit: a neighbor, someone from church, old friends. They sign in, and then, her family talks about it in the evening to refresh her memory of that visit.

The kitchen table is decorated with seasonal plastic tablecloths, like the one with big Easter eggs, and they keep Granny up to date. They talk to her about the greeting cards and photos that surround her. Her phone with huge keys sits next to her on the table with a list of numbers she could call, if she wanted to talk to someone. It doesn't matter that she can't remember to do that. They encourage her to answer the phone when it rings. When I call to ask if this is a good time to visit, it's often Granny who says "Hello. Who is this?" several times. Then when one of the Bettys gets on the phone and learns it's us, I hear her say, "Granny, it's your friend Jessie, the therapy dog. Would you like to have her come over now?"

"Oh, yes!" she answers.

"Okay, then here's the phone. You tell her you want her to come." And she does. I can see how much easier it would be for Betty to have answered the phone, told me to come and then told Granny I was on the way. I'm so touched by their care of her, the thoughtful and patient way they allow her to continue to live each day her way instead of doing the living for her. Granny makes her own choices.

One of the Bettys bragged on Granny one day, telling me that Granny had been a highly respected teacher in the community. She'd taught all of Betty's children. Granny smiled and pretended to remember that. Betty obviously shares our mantra: just for the moment. Granny is included in conversations and her opinion is asked. They let her decide where she will sit, what she'd like to do, what she'd like to eat, and if she'd like company, TV, or a nap.

She's forgotten most of her 103-year history. She moves slowly, repeats herself, and needs a lot of assistance. But, no one complains. They don't rush her, no one sees her as an inconvenience, and everyone is kind and patient. She's made to feel important and loved. They keep her bird feeders full and her flower gardens blooming, and everyone acts as if she'll always be here. They are talking about her next birthday two months away. They appreciate her every day and help her to make the most of every moment. She is truly respected and treated with dignity. I felt blessed to have experienced this.

"I'd like to have a dog like this one," she'd say when Jessie nuzzled her hand. "I think she likes lots of loving. I like that." They shared popcorn and when Granny's hand rested, Jessie reminded her to pet her some more.

I learned from watching this family care for Granny that respect and dignity are synonymous with love. Respect, dignity and love in every moment…could anyone ask for more? It's what Granny and Jessie shared.

JESSIE'S VIGIL

*W*e'd been visiting weekly at Granny's for four months when I had a message on my voice mail from someone in her family. The caller left her name and said she was kin of Granny and the message said: "...this message is for Jessie. Jessie, Granny said to tell you that she was feeling a little rundown and she's gone off to the hospital. She asked me to call you and tell you that she'd like you to drop by and see her at the hospital. Thanks, Jessie."

This particular hospital doesn't use therapy dogs. I called the administrator and explained the situation and he approved our visits. Jessie visited at Granny's hospital bedside everyday for the next week.

The first day, Granny said, "Now, have you done anything about fixing her hearing?" She remembered that Jessie was deaf. Everyone was surprised and rejoiced over that small victory over memory loss. The first few days, Granny rested her hand on Jessie's head and caressed her thick ears. She was relaxed, talked slowly to Jessie, and dozed. After that, Jessie's visits were more for the hospital staff, the two Bettys, and visiting family members. All of them seemed to want Jessie's silver and gold glitter all over them.

At the end of the week, Granny didn't wake up. We told her that Jessie was there, and Jessie sat silently at the bedside. Jessie, as I told you, is not the silent type. She is almost clownish with her happy little prance. She often emits some kind of sound. Even her feet on the floor make a merry little clicking noise. Whereas Lily can enter a room without a sound, Jessie announces herself gaily, tail waving. She doesn't usually sit when she goes for a visit. She stands throughout. She has a puppy's attention span and is always ready to go home–like most elderly.

But on that day, Jessie went to the head of Granny's bed and sat, mouth closed and quiet. She stared at a blank space on the wall above Granny's head. She was motionless for 30 minutes. Betty and I watched her, shrugged to each other, quietly wondering what she saw on the wall that we didn't see. When it was time to leave, Jessie was rooted to the spot and didn't seem to want to leave. Jessie is usually in a hurry to get into the car. But not today. Today, she wanted to look at the blank wall. She sat still as a stone, staring at that wall, while Granny slept.

At six o'clock the next morning, Jessie was at my bedside, paws on my pillow, nose in my face, whining and Jessie-talking. I gave her my most annoyed sigh and got up to let her out. She wouldn't go out. She paced and whined. *What does she want?* She wouldn't settle down, even though it was too early to be up. We ate, groomed, showered, and dressed. Jessie hung by the garage door, whining and chortling her funny noises.

I'd been thinking about Granny since I got up and since I had a full day planned with the golden rescue group decided to take Jessie for an early visit at the hospital. Jessie watched my every move and when I picked up my ID lanyard and her bandana, she bolted for the garage. She knew where she was going, and it seemed that was what she'd been asking for all along. She threw herself into the car, without assistance bad hips and all. She normally needs a boost.

It was eerie driving through town and up the mountain so early. No one was out yet on a Saturday morning and the shroud of fog was just lifting in the valley. The hospital parking lot was empty. Jessie jumped out of the car on her own and hurriedly pulled me through the doors. The reception area was still dark. She led me down the hall to Granny's room. She knew exactly where she was going and she was in a hurry to get there. Outside Granny's room, several people were gathered. A few I had met before, but the gentleman with the suit and tie, Bible in hand, I hadn't seen before. "Granny died at 6:15 this morning," Betty told me. I nodded. Jessie knew. I should have guessed.

I dropped the leash so Jessie could weave through the knot of people without me crowding, as everyone wanted to see her. She greeted everyone and then walked herself into the empty room. Granny was in the bed looking just as she had the day before, but everything else had been moved out of the room. None of her things were there–equipment, personal items, and furniture gone. Jessie sat down at the head of the bed, just as she had yesterday, silent and still, staring at the blank wall above Granny. In a minute, she jumped up and began vigorously sniffing the side of the mattress from the head to the foot. I don't think she missed a spot along the mattress edge. Her behavior was odd. I had no idea what she was doing. At the foot of the bed, she sat and looked up at me with her head cocked quizzically, ears perked. Her single whine sounded like a question. *What does she want? Does she understand this?* I bent down and looked in her wet eyes where little rusty stains were forming at the corners. I knew her deaf ears couldn't hear me, but I said, "Granny's gone, Jessie."

She bolted out of the room, leash dragging behind her. Her plumed tail was drooped and almost dragged on the floor. I'd never seen her tail down before. I didn't know she could do that. She ran passed everyone in the hall without a greeting and went straight out the automatic door. I hustled to catch up to the leash. Jessie always walks beside me, or lags a bit behind, but today she was leading the way in a hurry, with her leash dragging behind. She crossed the parking lot and I hit the car door remote in my pocket, opening the side door for her. She fell getting into the car. I had to scrape her up off the parking lot and lift her in. When we got home, she went straight to her bed and curled up, chin on her paws, quiet. She stayed there all day. Mostly, she was quiet, but off and on she emitted a soulful little crying sound from somewhere deep inside.

I don't know what any of this means. But there was a mysterious and beautiful connection, beyond my comprehension, between those two old souls. I'm of the opinion that there are things that we don't need to understand to appreciate. I've thought a lot about the ceremonial sniffing. Jessie collects things, a sock, a shoe, pajamas, and puts them on her bed and lays on them. When Dave leaves the house, she empties his closet of shoes, which she strews across her bed like puppies, and lays beside them. Maybe she just wanted something of Granny to take home with her and put on her bed where she collects her treasures? Was she collecting a remembrance of her old friend; a scent, something to keep? I don't know. What did she see on the wall behind Granny? What was she watching so intently? We will never know in this life.

What I do know is that Jessie brought some golden sunshine, a bit of fun, and some smiles to Granny in the final weeks of her very long life. That's Jessie's ministry as a therapy dog. But, there seems to have been a little more to it that none of us needs to understand.

For me, the blessings that I received at the other end of the leash will help me through some moments yet to come, as my own parents are 87 years young. I'll remember what I've learned, and their lives will be enriched because of Jessie's moments with Granny.

JESSIE'S RECONNECTING MOMENT

*S*ome weeks after Granny's departure, her family sent a gift to Jessie; a little remembrance of her old friend. A soft fleece pillow shaped like a dog bone, had been Granny's neck pillow. It supported her neck, while she watched TV. Perhaps she slept with it as well, I don't know. They thoughtfully placed it in a Ziplock bag and preserved the scent.

Catching Jessie alone on her bed, but awake, I gave her the pillow. She sniffed, sniffed, rolled it over, sniffed, sniffed. It was the caricature pose of golden joy, rear end in the air, tail waving and face rubbing the pillow. She smiled and rubbed both ears over and over on the pillow. Then she plopped down on top of it and rolled her shoulders all over it, her stiff old legs pedaling the air, remembering their limber puppy days. Her tongue lolled around her smiling lips. Her eyes were closed. She lay there a moment catching her breath, then rolled over. She positioned her little pillow between her shoulders and paws, tenderly laid her chin on it and went to sleep.

It was crystal clear to me that Jessie had just had the kind of reconnect moment that she usually brings to humans. She just reconnected with an old friend– just for a moment.

STAFF SOLACE

$\mathcal{E}$verywhere we visit, the staff is busy, overworked, and stressed. Being a caregiver can be exhausting and frustrating, both physically and emotionally, and paperwork can be just as tiring as machine work. I've seen how far-reaching pet therapy really is.

The staff and volunteers at the free dental clinic look forward to Jessie's visit. They say that Wednesdays are their best days, even though it's one of their busiest, because Jessie is there. Every member of the staff takes time out to come to the lobby and love on Jessie. They hug her and stroke her and joke about their own blood pressure dropping. Just seeing her seems to rejuvenate them and refresh their purpose for being there. Jessie rides on their parade float at Christmas and is one of their volunteer tooth fairies with her own set of little blue fairy wings for the parade and school visits. She's there for the staff as well as for the patients.

At a long-term care center we visit, the director is in a wheelchair like most of the patients. She's always delighted to see Lily and comes wheeling down the hall-way with arms outstretched. She greets me, but her concentration is on Lily. She pets and coos, nuzzles and caresses. Just like her patients, she seems to draw strength from Lily's strong, soft body.

At the largest hospital we visit, I'm surprised that all the staff knows Lily by name. In the two units that we visit weekly that would be expected, perhaps. But walking down the passageways and crossing the parking lot, doctors, nurses, technicians, and maintenance staff approach us and call out her name. It's like walking Miss Congeniality on a leash. They all want to pet her, talk to her, tell her about their own pets, thank her for coming, while feeling refreshed. "This just makes my day," many of them say.

One morning, a nurse came around the corner towards us. She squatted in front of Lily and wrapped her arms around her neck, not saying anything. I heard a little sniffling and when she finally stood up, there were tears on her cheeks.

"I'm so glad you came today. This has been a really bad day." She blew her nose, smiled, patted Lily, and with dignity restored, continued on with her duties.

A physician's assistant visited with us in ICU. When the P.A. bent over, her stethoscope thumped Lily's head. It was funny and we laughed about it, but the P.A. was really up-close-and-personal with Lily by that time. The stethoscope was off and Lily was into hugging and, surprisingly, kissing. She isn't normally a kisser and I was nervous about what the P.A. might think about that. She loved it. Then, she looked at me and said, "She knows."

Yes, probably, I thought, but I didn't. *Know what?* They petted and hugged, and with red-rimmed eyes, she said, "It was only a week ago, I had to put my 14 year-old dog down. I miss him so much. He used to kiss me just like that. I kid myself thinking I'm over it, but I'm not. This feels so good. I love you, Lily. Kissy?" She touched her chin and Lily responded. Somehow, Lily knew that a kiss on the chin was needed, even though she is not a kisser. She very rarely kisses.

The student nurses adore her. "This just makes their day," their supervisor told me. "It's a breath of fresh air for all of us, a quick break to a better world, then back to work."

Both maintenance men who replace the light bulbs at the hospital and rehab center climb down their ladders to see Lily and talk to her. One of them usually has a little surprise tucked in his pocket for her. They smile when they see her, and call to her.

At the nursing homes, the aides, orderlies, clerks, and housekeeping staff know and love Lily and Jessie and pause in their duties for a little love, drawing strength to continue, and refreshing their smiles.

A director of nursing told me, "The response people have to her is wonderful. Why, just having her in the room makes a difference. Can anyone look at her and not smile? In all my years of nursing and hospice care, I've met a lot of wonderful therapy dogs. I've never seen one interact so cheerfully and instinctively. She just brightens the day for everyone."

Lily accompanies me to my college classroom. Students cross the lawn and come in from the hall for a Lily hug or to pat her on the head and tell her about their dog at home that they miss so much. These are big strapping, healthy, athletic young people. One young man got all choked up telling me that his golden back home still slept on his empty bed. "This feels so right," he said while hugging my dog tightly. "Thanks." Yes, that's therapy, too.

Smile therapy isn't just for the elderly, the ill, the frail, the dying. It's also for those in good health who work hard, and play hard. Life's tough. A smile can make a huge difference for everyone. A smile is what a therapy dog can guarantee, and it's for everyone.

SIGNS OF THE TIMES

For the past few springs, the program director at the assisted living facility has asked for a specific visit in the spring. She likes both dogs to come. I dress in a 1912 Easter outfit and we dance to *"The Easter Parade."* This is an old routine from a few years ago when we competed in freestyle.

The costume is pretty to look at, though not necessarily comfortable for someone who lives in jeans and accessorizes with dog hair. It's yellow and has all the feminine draping, blue cummerbund, dotted Swiss and all. The huge hat's covered with yellow roses and blue forget-me-nots. The dogs' leashes are wrapped in yellow rose buds. They wear collars of big yellow roses, all very Fifth Avenue, 1912. It won a costume award and we earned a brace title with our Easter Parade routine.

The first year we did this, one of the residents told me that she remembered seeing just such a dress and her photos of her mother showed dresses just like this one.

"That's real nice," she said, and I knew she was thinking of her mom at that moment. Perhaps it's in a photo album in her attic of memories?

Our Easter Parade dance is very simple and is more of a choreographed promenade. The dogs switch sides and twirl around looking pretty. We get all the residents up to strut with us: wheelchairs, walkers, canes, everyone can be in our Easter Parade. We bring Easter bonnets and glittery top hats for everyone to wear. We have fun with it. I love how easily old folks can laugh at themselves and be silly. They're a lot like children in that respect–or dogs.

That whole routine is in a big plastic bag in the attic–until assisted living needs another Easter Parade. Isn't it interesting how many of life's moments end up in the attic or the cedar chest? Battle ribbons, trophies, photos, corsages–they're all there, along with the snake skins we shed when we moved on to the next phase of life. I imagine that Little Buddy's hospital bracelet will be taped into his scrapbook and one day, when he's somebody's grandpa, he'll find it in his attic. He'll laugh and say, "I remember when I was a frightened little guy in the hospital. There was a great moment when I saw a big dog grinning down at me and I forgot I was afraid." One day, Jessie's and Lily's collars and tags will be in the attic, too, with their trophies, ribbons, certificates, photos, and scrapbooks.

I'm not sure how we're going to pull this off this year. They really want to see Jessie. She doesn't go out very often anymore. Like many in assisted living, she's deaf and a little forgetful. She gets flustered and wants to go home. She needs help to get into the car. She prefers her familiar territory now, with less confusion.

I watch a lot of the old "doo wop" entertainers on Public TV. Have you noticed how it's awkward when a member of a group is suddenly *too* old, and the group will never be the same? We're there.

We might just dress up and walk around to the music this year; music that Jessie won't hear. No one will mind–or notice. They'll enjoy us because we're there paying attention to them and sharing a happy moment. None will remember seeing this last year. Most won't remember it this year, either. We'll offer them a diversion, a laugh, when the dogs roll around on the rug kicking their feet in the air, showing off for them. It's all just for that moment—that one particular, all important moment in life that is *now*. And therapy dogs will be there in that moment, present at the bedside of the sick and dying, their heads in the laps of the lonely or confused, sharing joy with the children, making difficult situations easier with their remarkable gifts.

LaVergne, TN USA
22 October 2010
201970LV00005B/1/P